NATIONAL
CENTER
FOR
**NONPROFIT
BOARDS**

T0107091

The National Center for Nonprofit Boards (N(dedicated to increasing the effectiveness of n(strengthening their boards of directors. Through i NCNB:

■ provides solutions and tools to improve boar(
■ acts as conveyer and facilitator in the development of knowledge about boards
■ promotes change and innovation to strengthen governance
■ serves as an advocate for the value of board service and the importance of effective governance.

NCNB is a 501(c)(3) nonprofit organization. To learn more about NCNB's publications, workshops, and consulting services, write us at 1828 L Street, NW, Suite 900, Washington, DC 20036-5104 or call 800-883-6262. Visit our website at www.ncnb.org or e-mail us at ncnb@ncnb.org.

AMHERST H.
WILDER
FOUNDATION
ESTABLISHED 1906

The Amherst H. Wilder Foundation is one of the largest and oldest endowed human service and community development organizations in America. For more than 90 years, the Wilder Foundation has been providing health and human services that help children and families grow strong, the elderly age with dignity, and the community grow in its ability to meet its own needs.

To learn more about the Amherst H. Wilder Foundation, write to 919 Lafond Avenue, Saint Paul, MN 55104 or call 800-274-6024 or visit www.wilder.org.

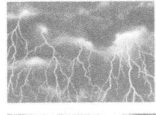

Contents

Why Conflict Happens

Introduction

Participating on a board of directors of a local nonprofit organization is, for many people in our communities, their most intimate experience with governance and democracy. There are 1.5 million nonprofits in the United States, and the number of people who participate in governance ranges between 4 million and 30 million. As Cyril O. Houle says in his book, *Governing Boards*, "Boards do not talk much about democracy. They do not need to do so. They are living proof of it."

The democratic process relies on debate, and sometimes conflict, between people with different views to bring out all aspects of public issues and to craft solutions to public problems. Likewise, nonprofit boards need debate, and sometimes conflict, to bring out the innovative and unique solutions to societal problems nonprofits work to ameliorate.

Despite the need for healthy conflict, the board can only make progress as a unified body. Individual board members have no authority in the nonprofit separate from the board. Members of boards serve without compensation, during their personal time, offering their professional skills and personal resources. Is it any surprise that conflicts might occur in a group of volunteers, working as a team in partnership with a paid professional staff, in an environment of constant change, diversity, limited resources, and demands for innovation? It is a testament to the integrity, will power, and vision of the people involved in nonprofits that so much important work gets done and organizations run as smoothly as they do.

As long as there are unique, creative, and passionate people leading nonprofit organizations in a constantly changing environment, there will be conflict. The job of board and staff leadership is to guide this inevitable conflict to constructive ends.

This booklet is primarily written for board chairs and chief executives as partners. It is frequently this pair who must manage conflict in nonprofits. This booklet offers a process that can

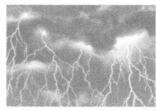

help nonprofit boards turn negative disputes into constructive processes that foster responsive, innovative, ethical, and productive nonprofit organizations and effective nonprofit boards — the best of democracy.

A Cautionary Tale of Two Boards

Conflict on a board — or elsewhere — is frequently considered a bad situation. Few people enjoy the feelings of anger, anxiety, and threat that frequently accompany it. However, conflict in its own right, without these accompanying negative attributes, is something valued in American society. It is often framed as competition, commonly viewed as a means to motivate achievement and as the basis for our economic system. It also exists in the forms of debate and compromise that create the cornerstone of our democratic process. New inventions, great art, or innovations of any kind would not be created if someone or something were not in some kind of tension or conflict. Change of all kinds is motivated by different views. In the nonprofit world, change is constant and essential. What does this have to do with boards? Quite a lot, as the following tale of two boards will illustrate.

The boards about to be described are both working boards of directors of real nonprofits. They are not dysfunctional boards. They are not rubber stamp boards that have abdicated their leadership role, nor are they the dreaded micromanagers. They are made up of skilled and intelligent members, who basically understand their roles as board members of nonprofit organizations. These boards are trying to oversee their organizations prudently, with commitment, generosity, and goodwill, adhering to the guidelines for the activities of effective nonprofit boards. However, the level of conflict on these boards strongly influences their own effectiveness and the success of the organizations they govern.

THE TOO-HARMONIOUS BOARD

This board of 16 oversees a large museum on the East Coast. The organization is more than 50 years old and owns a large building and an important collection. Its members are all ardent supporters of the museum and have an avid personal interest in the field the museum serves. All have served on the board between 3 and 15 years and have been generous with their time, connections, and personal wealth. The board has excellent attendance at its monthly meetings, where it conducts board business and has lunch together. The board has several hard-working subcommittees; a particularly active and successful one is the fund-raising committee. Members are close in age, and many are professionals or business leaders who have retired in the past five years. They get along well and are satisfied with their chief executive, whom they hired four years ago upon the retirement of the previous chief executive of 15 years. The chief executive in turn has a fairly stable, hard-working, and dedicated staff. There are the usual number of turf battles among departments and programs, but nothing out of the ordinary.

It would seem that this is as close to nirvana as a board can come, but something is not going well. Over the past five years, museum attendance has been dropping steadily. Neither new marketing efforts nor focusing on tourism has been effective in changing this trend. Several important funders have cut back or cut off funding to the museum. The board is baffled about why, when everything internally seems to be working so smoothly, the visitors and philanthropic community are becoming less supportive of this fine institution.

This is a board that is so harmonious that it has become complacent. The board loves, supports, and appreciates its museum for the treasure it is and sees no need for change. Yet the visitors see it as a rather archaic and static place. Guests are put off by the old-fashioned cases and mountings and the lack of interactive programming. Funders have had conversations with the development staff noting the need for changes in the programming and presentation, but the chief executive and board don't take reports of these conversations too seriously.

This board, because it is so harmonious, is far less inclined to innovate and take risks in running its museum than a board with genuine and constructive conflict would be. This museum is in no danger of closing its doors. The museum has an en-

dowment, and its generous board and their fund-raising efforts will keep the museum afloat financially for a while. However, until either a crisis or new people with fresh ideas challenge this board (stirring up a little conflict along the way), the organization will remain lackluster, and support from both the community and philanthropic organizations will continue to erode. Conflict, in the constructive sense, is just what is needed to revitalize this museum and its board.

THE EMBROILED BOARD

At the other extreme is a small grassroots human services organization that is so caught up in destructive conflict that there is no time or energy left for the board to truly lead the organization.

This board is made up of 12 individuals, most of whom also do volunteer work with the organization. Each board member is a successful professional in his or her own field. All of them are community-minded and politically active. Although this organization is nonpolitical in mission, the members bring their political agendas to the table. They are so busy disagreeing with the members who belong to other political parties that they form voting blocks around practically every issue brought before the board. Attendance at meetings is spotty, and a lot of grandstanding and interpersonal sniping goes on during meetings.

At the price of migraine headaches, the chief executive manages to keep the organization on course and generally gets the board to act upon immediate organizational needs. Despite what she knows about what the board *should* do, she is inclined to assign them as little work as possible. She does not even consider having them work on long-range planning or program evaluation — both much needed by the organization. The annual budget approval process is a nightmare. No matter how well the budget is prepared, the approval process is impeded by all the coalitions, interpersonal conflicts, and intrigues among board members.

In addition, because of the endless negotiation among board factions, most policy decisions become bland and meaningless. The staff feels that the board provides no guidance. As a result, different staff members interpret the board's policies differently, creating confusion and frustration for the organization's clients and conflict among the staff.

At this point the chief executive is thinking hard about moving on, and the word is out that the organization will be in trouble without her. This board is so embroiled in its conflicts that it is not aware that the chief executive is likely to leave nor that the organization's reputation is plummeting.

The point of these two tales is this: too little conflict on a board and an organization becomes stagnant, too much destructive conflict and it loses sight of its mission. For an organization to be vibrant and innovative, constructive conflict — differing perspectives, questioning of the status quo, and lively debate — are needed. When board members question and debate each other, it can be easy to slip from constructive conflict to a destructive type, in which people rather than problems are scrutinized and judged and people forget to disagree respectfully. It helps if board members understand the nature of conflict and how to use it constructively. It is essential for the board chair to know how to help manage and resolve conflicts that become destructive.

Nonprofits are Natural Places for Conflict to Occur

Just as the shape of a sailboat and the materials from which it is built affect its speed and performance, the structure of a nonprofit and the elements from which it is built affect conflict within it. The nonprofit's chief executive, board, staff, volunteers, clients, regulators, and funders all shape the organization. Each individual and group brings different assets and concerns. These differences are frequently the source of conflicts — turf battles between staff members, power struggles between board members or between board and staff, frustrations or secretiveness between foundations and nonprofits, or arguments about program implementation or data collection between government contractors and nonprofit service providers. Precisely because decision making and implementation are dispersed among so many different people, there is a potential for conflict over what things get done, how they get done, and who does them.

Besides the many internal and external forces that affect how a nonprofit does its work, two additional characteristics unique to nonprofits strongly influence conflict and how it is handled. First, leadership is shared between the board and the chief executive. Second, nonprofits are expected to be utopian agencies that are somehow above conflict.

Shared leadership inevitably raises the possibility of conflict. A board is made up of diverse people with diverse expectations. Board members from other sectors often have goals or methods that differ from those of nonprofit chief executives and staff, the lines of authority are often unclear, and the board is made up of part-time volunteers while the chief executive is a full-time, paid professional. The contexts for conflict are numerous and often stem from some of the same qualities that make the nonprofit sector so exciting and dynamic.

Diverse participation. In recent years nonprofits and the foundations that fund them have worked hard to find board members who accurately represent the diverse communities that the nonprofits serve. Though a multiplicity of viewpoints, experience, and expertise offers great benefits, it also increases the potential for disputes, debates, and full-blown battles.

Varied professional backgrounds. Boards often draw their membership from people whose work experience is in other sectors. Many conflicts on boards and between boards and executives result from the introduction of practices and values appropriate to other sectors but incompatible with nonprofits' legal and ethical foundations. In addition, boards are composed of professionals from different areas of expertise, all of whom see organizational issues from their own professional perspectives. Attorneys see legal issues, accountants see financial concerns, marketing experts use the marketing lens. Often they see the same issue differently, which can be an asset to the organization when the differing perspectives are respected and used. But sometimes different viewpoints can lead to conflict if a professional's perspective is narrow or devalues differing ones.

Role confusion between chief executive and board members. By law, a board of directors is collectively the captain of a nonprofit, and possesses the ultimate responsibility for its leadership. The board employs the chief executive, who reports to it. The chief executive is the person who deals with all the daily issues, who is held accountable, and whose career is tarnished if problems hurt the organization. When something goes wrong in a nonprofit it is most frequently the chief executive and staff who handle the problem and whose reputations are on the line. Most boards of nonprofits remain invisible and unaccountable. The reason for this lies in the vagueness of board leadership. Though the board is legally chartered to steward the organization on behalf of the community at large, its members may be unclear about their responsibilities, and accountability for the quality of the board's leadership is nearly nonexistent. As a result, the level of stewardship provided by a board can range from lackadaisical to micromanagerial — either one a recipe for conflict. In addition, as board leadership and composition change, the lines of authority and responsibility are also likely to change. This continual redefinition of leadership roles is built into the structure of nonprofit organizations. The dynamic of a part-time volunteer board managing a full-time professional executive holds the potential for many conflicts.

Conflict management by a nonprofit leader working in this context has limits, pressures, and responsibilities that differ significantly from those of external conflict mediators.

The nature of volunteer work. Board members are part-time volunteers, which makes it nearly impossible for them to be as knowledgeable about the organization, its environment, and its services as the staff may be. Though boards have ultimate responsibility for the nonprofit, they provide guidance on a limited and intermittent basis. Board members rely heavily on the chief executive to keep everything on course and running smoothly, to educate and advise them, and to oversee the actual workings of the organization.

The challenge of establishing a unified organizational vision. One of the key roles of a board, with the aid of its staff, is to establish a unified vision and mission for the organization. Many boards resist this work, as it seems less pragmatic and more time-consuming than overseeing the functional operations of the organization. However, without a clear, well-understood vision, the actors in a nonprofit — both board members and staff — work toward their own vision of what the organization is to do. These often unstated and differing visions can pull the organization in different directions, creating conflicts for board and staff.

The second unique feature of nonprofit organizations that affects conflict is the expectation of a utopian work environment — one that is above conflict. Nonprofits attract creative, dedicated people who work long hours for modest compensation and usually believe ardently in their organization's mission. Rightfully, they believe that through their work in the nonprofit organization they personally contribute to the good of others. To a degree, they draw their identity from the work and reputation of the nonprofit for which they work.

Ironically, nonprofit employees' creativity, individuality, and passion make them likely candidates for conflict. Their positive view of their work and themselves as good people doing good work leads them to assume that they will be *above* discord. Because of this belief, many conflicts are buried and ferment until they surface again as complex and emotion-laden disputes.

This same attitude exists on nonprofit boards. Board members give of their time, expertise, and personal resources to support a cause in which they believe. This is good work and the basis of true democracy. The same sense of good people doing good work exists on nonprofit boards — and it has the same effect.

In addition to expecting themselves to be above conflict, nonprofit employees often expect that the administration and management of a nonprofit will be better — less formal and more inclusive, entrepreneurial, and personal — than their counterparts in other sectors. Many nonprofit workers also expect that the nonprofit sector itself will provide a more flexible, informal, and egalitarian work environment than other sectors. While this is sometimes true, many employees are disappointed to find that nonprofits can be rigid and hierarchical and bound by rules, policies, procedures, and precedents — all of which thwart their expectations of being free to do things their own way. Likewise, board members often come to board service expecting camaraderie, consensual decision making, and a singular vision of service to the organization — they too are often disappointed.

Whether someone serves a nonprofit as a volunteer or professional leader, he or she assumes many roles, some of which are contradictory. The individual may at times find himself or herself acting as a steward and advocate for the organization; at other times as a guide, problem solver, and advocate for staff; or as an advocate and activist for the community and the issues the organization addresses. Conflict management by a nonprofit leader working in this context has limits, pressures, and responsibilities that differ significantly from those of external conflict mediators who enter the organization for a short time to help with a particular issue and who have no special obligations to the organization nor ongoing relationships with the people in it. Being cognizant of these limits, pressures, and responsibilities will help a leader decide when and how to handle conflict himself or herself and when to seek external assistance.

What the nonprofit leader needs is a practical guide for handling the natural conflicts that arise as a board and staff members guide a nonprofit in its work. These conflicts can range from the simplest difference of opinion to complex, long-standing contentions involving serious issues and many parties. This booklet presents basic information that can be immediately applied to board conflicts. Its goals are to

■ help nonprofit board members understand some of the basic elements of conflict,

■ provide an orderly way to think through and address conflicts, and

■ offer additional resources for readers interested in more information about conflict and its management.

Typical Points of Conflict in Nonprofits

Differences among board members in
■ Personal and communication styles
■ Vision for the organization
■ Personal expectations of the organization
■ Levels of participation in board work
■ Understanding of board members' roles
■ Amount of loyalty to the executive and the organization
■ Specific professional perspectives and areas of expertise

Areas of authority and responsibility divided between executive and board
■ Means of accountability for chief executive to the board
■ Degree of autonomy available to the chief executive in decision making and action
■ Amount of information the board needs to feel informed and work effectively
■ Level of policy making in which the board engages
■ Level of financial responsibility the board undertakes to keep the organization solvent

Areas of authority and responsibility between the board and its auxiliary groups
■ Subcommittees' roles and authorities
■ Auxiliary groups' roles and authorities
■ Conflicting missions and needs among interdependent boards or groups

Areas of authority and responsibility between board chair and executive
■ Spokesperson role for organization
■ Amount of information the chair needs
■ Evaluation of the executive's performance

Level of staff access to the board
■ Budget allocations between programs
■ Personnel issues and grievances

Differences among staff
■ Management styles
■ Methods of program implementation
■ Allocation of time and resources
■ Personal and communication styles
■ Expectations for participation in decision making
■ Worker expectations for autonomy

Board Conflicts

Board conflicts are among the most challenging conflicts a chief executive faces. They generally come in two forms — conflicts among board members and conflicts between the board and management of the organization, either the chief executive or the staff. Both of these difficult situations require special consideration.

When it comes to board conflicts of either kind, it is the role of the board chair to lead in managing the conflict. A chief executive should not take visible leadership in board conflicts because this may erode the confidence individual board members have in the chief executive's objectivity in working with the board. In addition to setting the agenda and managing board meetings, the board chair has an essential role as a facilitator of communication and healer of miscommunications on the board. At the board table, the chair can facilitate discussion so that disagreements are directed at the issue at hand and not at individuals. Away from the table, a chair often uses informal communications to mend differences among members or clarify miscommunications. In these efforts, the chief executive can support the chair but cannot fulfill the chair's role.

When Conflict Occurs on the Board

Conflict Among Board Members

It is a rare board chair or chief executive who relishes conflict. Though most value board members' constructive disagreements about what is best for the organization, they dread the times when these disagreements become destructive, and it does not take much for disagreements to slip over the line from constructive to destructive. Many board members also dislike conflict, so much so that they frequently abdicate their board responsibilities rather than deal with them.

A recent study of the members of more than 50 boards in Minnesota found that most people join boards to "network, make friends, and do good." The study also reported that avoiding conflict is the most common reason for members' resignations. It is not uncommon for half the membership of a board to resign or just drift away from a board as a significant conflict unfolds. This loss of valuable leadership and talent drains the nonprofit's resources. Time and money must be spent to recruit and orient new board members. In addition, resigning board members may cost the organization in contributions and reputation. For these reasons, it is imperative that a conflict be resolved with as many board members as possible remaining committed to the organization.

Both board chair and chief executive should play a role in resolving board conflict; however, each should play a different one. The board chair should serve as the facilitator and lead, while the chief executive may provide data and process advice. Mediating a conflict among board members holds a real danger for a chief executive. He or she frequently ends up caught in the emotional crosscurrents between warring bosses — set up to lose no matter what the outcome. In a board conflict, it is nearly impossible for a chief executive to maintain each board member's belief in his or her impartiality. Some board members will inevitably

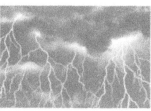

believe that the chief executive is somehow manipulating the situation or will come to view him or her as an ally of the opposing party. True or not, these beliefs will erode the board's trust and confidence in the chief executive — the key factors for a successful working relationship between a chief executive and a board. A chief executive's role should be one of gathering helpful information, recommending options for conflict resolution processes, and coaching the board chair.

Even if a chief executive has strong ideas about the issues dividing a board, it is wise to let the board chair take the lead in resolving conflicts within the board. After all, managing the board *is* the chair's job, and a large part of that job is facilitating constructive discussion and decision making by the board, and keeping channels of communication open among board members. This role also includes helping board members reopen constructive discussion and decision making when negative conflict has occurred. Unfortunately, many chairs do not understand or accept the full scope of their responsibilities. Some would rather not deal with conflict even when they understand it is their role.

The Emotional Element

One factor that contributes to the challenge of handling board conflicts is the emotional rancor that often occurs. A discussion that begins as a difference in members' views on a business issue can quickly become intense and personal. Some board members make personal attacks or embarrass others as they argue their points. The negative feelings created by public embarrassment perpetuate a dispute even when the conflict about the issue can be settled easily.

When exchanges get negative and personal, two things happen. The board members in conflict have increasing difficulty communicating constructively, and uninvolved board members become increasingly uncomfortable watching the negative exchanges. After a negative exchange at a meeting, a skilled chair will encourage the parties to resolve their issues away from the boardroom. On boards, as in other group settings, small conflicts left unresolved tend to simmer into a rich stew of resentment. Early intervention by the board chair can prevent this.

One of the most frequently used strategies in board conflicts is the private meeting. This is not done to keep the board conflict a secret, but rather for the comfort of the disputing parties and the uninvolved board members. To conduct a private meeting, the board chair can use shuttle diplomacy, speaking privately with individual board members. Or, he or she can bring a limited number of disagreeing members together privately for a facilitated discussion outside of the boardroom. This can be especially helpful when a conflict is among only a few of the board members. However, the number of members a chair can convene without the meeting becoming an official board meeting is affected by the quorum stipulations in an organization's bylaws. If the number of people involved in the conflict constitutes a quorum, a meeting of all of them will be a formal meeting of the board and all members should be invited to attend. If uninvolved members know the meeting topic in advance, they can choose whether to attend, but they should not be excluded.

When a conflict that includes loss of face erupts in a board meeting and is then resolved privately, the uninvolved members who witnessed the confrontation need to know that it has been resolved. Otherwise, they may be confused or believe that important decisions are being made behind their backs. The board chair can simply state that the problems between the disagreeing members have been cleared up without providing details.

Possible Resources

Whether it is the board chair or a facilitator from outside the board who takes the lead as conflict manager, the chief executive's role must be to assist and coach that person. It is not surprising to find board leaders uncomfortable with conflict and its management. Remember, few people enjoy or expect to have to resolve conflict as their contribution to the work of a nonprofit organization. The power relationship between a chief executive and

the board, as well as the impossibility of the chief executive being perceived as neutral, argues strongly against the chief executive serving as the conflict manager.

When a board chair is willing to serve as the conflict manager, willingly or even hesitantly, the organization is best served. A chief executive should support the chair emotionally and coach him or her on conflict analysis, process design, and other skills. No matter how much analysis or coaching a chief executive provides, however, the board chair must take the lead in managing the conflict. A more comprehensive discussion of these skills is available in *Resolving Conflicts in Nonprofit Organizations* (Angelica 1999).

If a board chair, even with support and coaching, is unwilling or unable to manage a conflict, he or she should, in consultation with the chief executive, seek another leader. A vice chair might fill this role, although members may ask why the chair is not managing the conflict. This can undermine the chair's authority, and should be avoided. A highly respected past board chair or board member can be a good choice. Whoever is chosen, the person should be trained in conflict management, well-regarded by all the parties, viewed as impartial toward the parties, and objective about the issues.

If neither current nor past board leaders are willing or able to manage the conflict, consider using a skilled mediator. For information on finding and choosing a mediator, see Finding External Help with Conflict Resolution on page 38.

Conflict Between Board and Chief Executive or Staff

Conflicts among members are not the only conflicts that come to a board. The board also serves as an internal court of last resort for other organizational conflicts. Conflicts between the chief executive or other staff and the board are extremely sensitive. First, a significant power imbalance exists because the board is the chief executive's employer. Second, the chief executive is the bridge between the board and staff and must understand and represent these groups' differing viewpoints to each other. This task can be delicate and precarious.

Conflict Between Board and Chief Executive

A chief executive can wind up in conflict with the board in three ways: when staff conflict is brought to the board, when direct conflict exists between the chief executive and some or all of the board members, and when a staff person makes an end run, bypassing the chief executive and bringing an issue to the board or to individual members.

When Staff Conflict Is Brought to the Board

A staff conflict brought before the board can ensnare the chief executive, causing him or her to lose the board's confidence. To the board, the chief executive represents staff leadership and is responsible for maintaining staff productivity and harmony. Given this, board members tend to regard staff conflicts brought to them as an indication of a deficiency in the chief executive's management skills. Board members often resent having to manage staff conflicts — after all, they did not donate their personal time to resolve staff battles.

Even so, the board *should* step in when efforts to resolve a conflict at the staff level have not succeeded. It is an appropriate and necessary role for a board to serve as the "court of last resort" within the organization. When the chief executive brings a staff conflict to the board, he or she should outline the nature of the problem and explain the process the board can use to resolve it. The chief executive should bring any information about the conflict resolution process as it is affected by union contracts or the organizational bylaws, as well as rules covering special issues like harassment or abuse complaints if such issues are involved. If the issue requires confidentiality, the chief executive should explain the organization's obligation to maintain confidentiality.

Often the executive committee or personnel committee of the board assumes the role of hearing and resolving staff conflicts that come before the board. If an organization's bylaws or the charters of its committees authorize the personnel or executive committee to handle conflicts, the chair should activate one of these committees. If not, encourage the board to delegate the task to one of these two committees. There are three reasons for this. First, the use of a committee gives the organization two chances for internal conflict resolution before turning to an outside organization — first through the committee, and then through the full board if necessary. Second, the use of a committee limits the dissemination of information about the conflict, keeping it more confidential. Finally, the use of a committee frees the rest of the board to attend to the organization's other important business. The chief executive should serve as a resource and support for the committee chair who is handling the conflict.

It is important that the full board understand the role of the committee and support it. If the full board second-guesses its committee, a second conflict is likely to occur — this one among board members. This is not as unlikely as one would think, because it is not unusual for staff to lobby board members who may not serve on the committee, or for non-committee members to be curious about the conflict details and seek out information from staff. It would be wise for the chief executive to discuss the process with the whole board to give them confidence in the method by which the committee will seek to develop a resolution and to alert them to potential pitfalls, such as staff lobbying or the board undermining the process through second-guessing the committee's work. If uninvolved board members don't fully understand why it is prudent for only a few board members to know the full details of the conflict, they can feel excluded. Also, the full board should be told the outcome of the conflict (not the details) and its implications for the organization.

The committee conflict resolution process involves several activities. The committee designs a process, hears from all the parties, and helps generate and test potential solutions. However, the committee also serves as arbitrator, developing a resolution it believes is best for the organization and the parties in conflict. Depending on the bylaws or charter of the committee, the decision can either stand as decided or need to be ratified by the entire board. If the people in the conflict are still unsatisfied, they can turn to the full board for a hearing before seeking external assistance.

When Board and Chief Executive Are in Direct Conflict

When a chief executive is in serious direct conflict with the board, he or she usually loses, and may resign or be fired. Occasionally the whole board resigns, and the chief executive establishes a new board that supports him or her. Frequently a board is split into factions for and against. These factions create a dual conflict — a chief executive and board conflict, and a conflict among board members. In any case, the organization usually loses momentum, continuity, expertise, and leadership. Additionally, a conflict resolved by either the board or chief executive leaving is likely to cost the organization money, the confidence of its staff, and its good name — perhaps its most valuable asset. (Of course there are times when an ineffective chief executive should be removed, but this action should be taken by the board only after documented performance evaluations and demonstrated efforts to help the chief executive remedy any weaknesses.)

Few conflicts between chief executives and boards erupt suddenly. Usually they are preceded by smaller conflicts that, if not handled well, erode the confidence or trust between the board and the executive. Handling small conflicts *when they occur* is important because once a direct conflict breaks out between board and chief executive, it is extremely difficult to resolve. Prevention is the best route — having clear expectations and roles for the chief executive and board, conducting regular performance evaluations for both, and developing clear policies for the organization stave off much potential for board/chief executive conflict.

When this type of conflict does develop, however, rapid action and professional help are called for. Clearly a chief executive cannot manage a significant conflict in which he or she is a party, and neither can the board chair. In this case an external resource is the best option. Some choices include

- a mediator,
- an organizational consultant with conflict management skills, and

- the organization's previous board chair, chief executive, or similar leader with conflict management skills.

When considering these resources for conflict management, be sure that they are viewed as unbiased by all parties.

> *Handling small conflicts when they occur is important because once a direct conflict breaks out between board and chief executive, it is extremely difficult to resolve.*

Many times, unfortunately, neither the chief executive nor the board chair and board are eager to use a conflict resolution process. Instead the conflict quickly becomes a battle of wills and wiles. Many nonprofit leaders hesitate to use conflict resolution processes in board/chief executive conflicts because people's identities are threatened and so much is at stake. The chief executive's livelihood, career, and professional reputation are jeopardized, and board members' identities as stewards with the ultimate authority in the organization are at risk. The two sides quickly become locked in a war of egos and wills.

This is precisely the type of situation where a neutral outsider can help, but nonprofit leaders must have enough knowledge about and confidence in the conflict resolution process — *in advance of needing it* — to know that the process can only help, not hurt, their situation. Awareness of conflict resolution skills and available resources can be introduced to board members as part of board orientation or training.

If the board and chief executive know about conflict resolution processes and, for the sake of the organization, are willing to try to mediate their conflict, they must first work together to select a mediator. Page 39 has a list of criteria for selecting a mediator. In this situation the key criterion is that the person be viewed as neutral. He or she can be someone all the parties already know and trust equally or someone previously unknown to the board and chief executive.

When Staff Makes an End Run

An end run occurs when staff members advocate or complain about organizational or personal issues to a board member or members without first working with the chief executive. This action establishes interpersonal dynamics and communication channels that invite conflict.

An example of an end run to a board occurred at a nonprofit day care center. A staff member who baby-sat for a board member's children complained that she did not get enough sick leave. This rather new employee had not accrued a great deal of leave and, unfortunately, like many new day-care workers, caught every illness being passed among the children. The board member, who was rather new herself, moved to greatly increase the number of sick leave days for new employees at a board meeting without ever talking to either the interim chief executive or the board chair. The board member made the motion as a goodwill gesture to the day-care worker, whom she liked. The interim director was furious because she knew that this staff person had argued with the recently departed chief executive and had used the opportunity to try to press her case. It took discussion at two additional board meetings to fully cover the effects such a decision would have on the organization's financial obligations and on staff morale before the end run was curtailed. This left the conflict between the interim director and employee yet to be dealt with.

It is important that both new employees and board members be told *during orientation* that the chief executive is the point person for the board of directors. In some larger organizations, staff members are not allowed to communicate with board members. In smaller and more informal organizations, there is often no such restriction — *but in all cases, the policy should be to keep the chief executive informed of any staff interaction with board members.*

When an end run *does* occur, the chief executive needs to talk with the board members and the staff involved about the board/staff communications policy. A naïve staff person is easily educated, but one who is unwilling to follow protocol is another matter. Staff who understand the way chief executives work with boards generally make end runs when they feel the chief executive isn't supporting them and believe all other avenues are closed. Because end runs are risky and put staff in direct conflict with the executive, a staff person has to be desperate or angry to take the chance. In general, this means the staff person and the chief executive are probably involved in an unresolved conflict. It's imperative to work through the conflict that motivated the staff member to risk an end run. A conflict such as this will likely require the assistance of a third party for resolution.

> *The board chair and chief executive are the people who must help the board better understand conflict and develop ways to disagree constructively — before serious conflicts erupt.*

It is also important to remind the staff person about expectations that he or she follow the organization's communication policy — and to discuss the consequences of disregarding the policy. This discussion should be documented. Disciplinary action (based on the written personnel policy) may be required, but it should be used sparingly because the goal is to set a positive tone for settling the dispute, not to fuel the fire.

It's equally imperative to immediately talk with the board members who were involved in the end run — about the substance of the concern raised by the staff member, how the chief executive is handling the conflict, and the problems created by not following existing communication policies. Don't be surprised if board members are unaware of the policy or the reasons it exists. It is natural for board members to want to be supportive and friendly toward the organization's staff. It can be hard for some people to determine when this friendliness crosses professional boundaries and becomes detrimental to the organization, which must be their topmost concern.

A chief executive's or board chair's first goal is to get the conflict off the board table until the chief executive and the staff person have made an effort to work through the conflict. (This is a situation where the board chair can serve as a third party or facilitator.) Depending on a board's policies and on its initial involvement in the conflict, the resolution of a staff conflict may be brought before the board for the board's information or approval. In any case, the involved board members should be alerted to how the conflict is being handled and its general resolution. A chief executive's second goal is to regain the trust of the board members involved. Honest communication is the best route to rebuilding confidence. A board chair can also help with this through discussions with the involved board member. If efforts away from the board table fail to resolve the conflict, the board chair should be the person to bring the conflict to the board for one of its committees to handle.

In cases such as these, board members often get upset that they are asked not to communicate directly with staff about problems in the organization and are encouraged to discuss any such information received with the chief executive and board chair. This seems to fly in the face of the strongly held American value of freedom of speech. But there are some limitations to freedom of speech when a person becomes a board member of a nonprofit. When a board establishes a policy or political stance, even members who may have opposed it during board discussion may not speak against it publicly once the board adopts it, unless they choose to leave the board. Confidentiality around personnel issues and other organizational circum-

stances also infringe on absolute freedom of speech. Likewise, keeping an organization's staff and board leadership fully informed requires that board members direct the discussion of organizational problems brought to them by staff to the organizational leadership. It is part of the role of each board member to encourage clear and direct communication within the organization. End runs lead to the proliferation of multiple channels of communication, secretiveness, misinformation, and ultimately conflict. This concept is often one that board members understand at their own workplace but sometimes lose sight of when serving on a board.

Given the inevitability of conflict in nonprofits, board members need to know how to make conflicts constructive. The board chair and chief executive are the people who must help the board better understand conflict and develop ways to disagree constructively — *before* serious conflicts erupt. Healthy conflict on a board can stimulate creativity and strengthen the organization. Training a board in the processes of healthy conflict is always a worthwhile investment of the organization's resources. Much of the information that follows is appropriate for use in board and staff training to help people both understand and handle conflict in positive ways.

What Conflict Looks Like

The Structure of Conflict

When people either find themselves in a conflict or trying to manage one, the conflict often seems quite chaotic. It is hard to understand why the people involved are saying and doing what they are. Conflict, much like chaos, however, does have structure and shape. Understanding the general structures and shapes that conflicts tend to follow can help make a given conflict more understandable and ultimately easier to manage.

Experts in conflict resolution have identified six categories of conflict, grouped by the types of issues around which they occur. The six categories are *relationship conflicts, identity conflicts, data conflicts, structural conflicts, value conflicts,* and *interest conflicts.* Recognizing these categories can help in analyzing conflicts and designing appropriate conflict resolution strategies.

RELATIONSHIP CONFLICTS

Relationship conflicts concern the way people view and treat one another. They are frequently based on miscommunication, repetitive negative behavior, stereotypes, or misperceptions. They always involve strong emotions. These conflicts often touch people's deepest feelings about themselves and others and cut to the emotional core of the people involved. Sometimes called *personality conflicts,* relationship conflicts are much broader than simple personality differences. In nonprofit organizations, relationship conflicts are often mixed with other types of conflict. Other conflicts may mask what are truly relationship conflicts. On boards, when members move from questioning or judging organizational issues to questioning or judging people, relationship conflicts are likely.

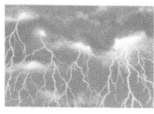

IDENTITY CONFLICTS

Identity conflicts occur when people sense that the essence of who they are has been attacked, belittled, or ignored. These are serious, difficult conflicts; resolving them takes a great deal of discussion and mutual education between parties. Identity conflicts are often based on racial, ethnic, gender, or religious differences. When the values, practices, or beliefs closely associated with a person's self or group identity are either attacked or dismissed, the people involved in the conflict have the tendency to dehumanize one another. As nonprofits are increasingly staffed by, are governed by, and work with people from many different cultures, identity conflicts are more common. Working with an identity conflict requires patience. It may be a long, slow process to resolution.

DATA CONFLICTS

Data conflicts are disagreements about information, its interpretation, its relevance, the procedures used to gather or analyze it, or any combination of these. Data conflicts happen when a nonprofit organization needs to justify funding based on certain data or when legislative or rules changes are being debated. One can arise when staff or board members interpret budgetary numbers differently, some seeing a cash flow issue and others a deficit.

Some advocacy-oriented nonprofits have found that questioning the validity of their opponent's data, providing new interpretations of it, or questioning the procedures used to collect it are effective ways to get the media to cover issues important to them or to delay undesirable decisions. They use data conflicts as a technique for drawing attention to their agenda.

Data conflicts can be about the actual data, how the data was collected, or how it will be applied. An example of a data conflict involving the actual data occurred when a local planning commission released figures about the effectiveness of septic systems. Environmental organizations used the data to emphasize the level of pollutants released by septic systems. Housing developers interpreted the same data with a positive spin, creating confusion for public officials.

STRUCTURAL CONFLICTS

Structural conflicts are about time, organizational or political structure, or proximity. Many organizational conflicts result from the organization's structural systems. Some structural conflicts are intentional, such as checks and balances between different parts of a nonprofit regarding the expenditure of money. Other structural elements unintentionally result in conflict, such as the differing fiscal years and budget planning cycles of funders and applicant organizations, conflicting deadlines for fund-raising drives, and procedures that reduce the work in one organizational unit while increasing it in others. Turf battles may be structural. Conflicts between an organization's main office and satellite offices are often structural, as are conflicts within boards about the responsibility and authority of subcommittees.

VALUE CONFLICTS

Value conflicts occur when one group of people tries to force its values or belief system on another. We see value conflicts in our communities today concerning issues such as abortion, censorship, and gay and lesbian rights. True value disputes are generally irresolvable and quite emotional. A person's values and beliefs are so much a part of his or her identity and self-worth that it's fruitless to try to change them or negotiate about them. Though people's values do change, they do so only when a person chooses to change them. This is most likely to happen when a person gets new, meaningful information that influences his or her ideas. In a value conflict people often feel strongly that they are right and others are wrong. Issues are often viewed and presented in black and white terms, with no gray areas allowed.

In true value conflicts, the only resolution is tolerance. People in these conflicts must simply accept that others' values are different and need not be changed. Disengagement is the usual resolution strategy. The results of disengagement without tolerance are miserable: They include segregation, dis-

crimination, xenophobia, ethnic cleansing, apartheid, and isolationism — all of which breed further dangerous and destructive conflicts.

Occasionally value disputes can be worked through if parties share a higher value than the disputed one. They can sometimes settle their differences by emphasizing their shared higher goals. At times this technique is applied in the creation of legislation, but the agreement often breaks down later when the subordinate values come back into play during rule making or implementation. In the case of a nonprofit, this higher value must be the organization's. Should a board or staff member find his or her organization's values unacceptable, he or she has two options — debate the value within the organization in an effort to change the organizational value, or leave the organization.

INTEREST CONFLICTS

Interest conflicts are about actual or perceived incompatible needs or desires. Interests are the underlying needs or compelling issues for each party in a dispute. They must be addressed for the parties to reach a mutually satisfactory agreement.

Interest conflicts abound, and most are resolvable. This type of conflict frequently has four components — each of which needs to be addressed for a long-lasting resolution. An interest conflict often includes *substantive* concerns about money, time, land, or other resources. There are also *procedural* concerns about how things get done or how decisions are made. There are *relationship* issues, like trust, respect, inclusion, friendship, and reciprocity. Finally, there are *identity* issues, which have to do with culture, religion, ethnicity, appearance, ability, or other personal characteristics; these often overlap with relationship issues. If a conflict resolution fails to meet any one of these needs, people may not be satisfied and the conflict will continue or resurface.

Constructively handled, interest conflicts can lead to innovation and creativity. In an organizational setting, interest conflicts are likely to occur as the budget is being developed, in the allocation of staff time among programs, in discussions about compensation, or during a planning process.

The Shape of Conflict

Not only are conflicts categorized, but there are several typical patterns they take as they develop. Any of the categories of conflict just described can take one of a number of shapes. The four most easily recognized shapes that conflict takes are *direct conflict, spiral conflict, subtle conflict,* and *violent conflict.*

DIRECT CONFLICT

Conflicts that are recognized and addressed by the disputing parties are called *direct conflicts.* This is the simplest pattern and one in which parties already share considerable information about the conflict. They often yield positive outcomes in terms of the solution to the problem at hand and the relationship between the individuals in conflict. Though most people do not look forward to confronting a conflict, people who have resolved a conflict often feel a positive bond. A forthright discussion of differing ideas about an annual budget, an organization's strategic plan, or a policy issue can be a direct conflict.

Understanding how people are influenced by their own histories with conflict can help when facing a board or staff conflict.

SPIRAL CONFLICT

Have you ever been in a situation where people seem forever at odds? As soon as one concern seems resolved, another one pops up. In such a *spiral conflict* the people involved frequently raise many issues but never get to their central concern, of which they may not even be aware. They literally spiral around the source of the conflict, getting sucked deeper and deeper as tensions, emotions, and frustrations escalate. Often it takes an outsider, possibly a new board member or organizational consultant, to help people see the issue around which they are spiraling. Occasionally people who *want* to remain in conflict engage in a spiral conflict. A spiral conflict may develop on a board when someone is passed over for a coveted chair position and subsequently finds fault with the actions of the person who was given the position.

SUBTLE CONFLICT

A *subtle conflict* is one in which at least one party refuses to acknowledge the conflict, even though the tension is palpable. It is common for the party who doesn't acknowledge the conflict to describe the party who does as oversensitive, imagining things, or whiny. Within nonprofits, a subtle conflict may be about poor performance by a well-loved staff or board member or a tradition or policy that is no longer appropriate to the current staff or organizational environment.

VIOLENT CONFLICT

It seems almost too obvious to state that *violence* — either physical or psychological — is a manifestation of conflict. Violent conflict in the nonprofit sector is evident in the bombing of Planned Parenthood clinics and the murder of doctors who perform abortions by those who disagree with their actions. Workplace conflict resulting in violence between employees or between management and employees is increasing as well. These are examples of the destructive shape that conflict can take.

How Individual Experience Affects Conflict

One can better understand conflict by looking at it through a variety of lenses. Thinking about the six categories and four shapes of conflict can help to sort out issues and understand how a conflict is playing out. However, other factors influence both the creation and the resolution of conflict, including temperament, personal experience, cultural background, and an individual's relationship with the dominant culture. Boards and staffs are made up of diverse individuals who bring their own specific experiences to the board table and workplace. Along with their goodwill, generosity, and professional expertise come their own personal histories, including their experiences with conflict. Understanding how people are influenced by their own histories with conflict can help when facing a board or staff conflict. In addition, each organization has its own culture, which also influences the experience of conflict. It is sometimes the practice in conflict-aversive organizations to "kill the messenger" who identifies a conflict. In such organizations, staff and board members quickly learn to push conflicts under the table, where they create all sorts of dysfunctional dynamics within the organization. Honestly considering whether the organizational culture is influencing conflict negatively is worth doing. Taking all these factors into account can further help bring a conflict to a constructive end.

How We Deal with Conflict

Each individual develops his or her own ways of dealing with conflict based on the family and social context in which he or she grew up. In addition, our own temperaments determine which conflict management style we find most comfortable. We tend to develop at least two — a preferred style and a backup style. Our preferred style is what we use when we are calm and feel in control. Our backup style is often the one we use under stress or when our preferred style has been unsuccessful. Most of us are familiar with the styles that we prefer, but we frequently do not understand (or else undervalue) the other styles. The ideal, of course, is for each of us to be able to use many different styles, depending on the situation at hand.

Each conflict management style has its own strengths and limitations. Recognizing them can help a board chair or chief executive develop a successful strategy for resolving conflict between individuals with different styles, in the same way that understanding differences in people's thinking processes or work styles can help build a board or staff into an effective team.

In the 1970s, Kenneth W. Thomas and Ralph H. Kilmann developed an assessment tool widely used to help people understand their own and others' behavior regarding conflict. They theorized that, when facing a conflict, people use five major styles of behavior — competing, accommodating, avoiding, compromising, and collaborating.

Competing behavior: a style in which a person addresses his or her own concerns with little regard for the concerns of others. It is frequently associated with the use of power, winning for its own sake, or defending a position believed to be right. It can be useful in emergencies, when quick decisions are vital, and when making decisions about unpopular courses of action, such as instituting discipline, layoffs, or budget cuts in organizations. Competing behavior can be effective when the people involved are not likely to be in a relationship in the future.

Accommodating behavior: a style in which a person neglects his or her own concerns to satisfy those of other people. It can be associated with self-sacrifice and selflessness or with lack of assertiveness or fear. It is useful when a concern is of much greater importance to one party than another. It is often used when preserving harmony is essential. People also use accommodating behavior to establish social credit for future payback, as in "I'll scratch your back if you scratch mine."

Avoiding behavior: a style in which a person does not address his or her own concerns or those of other people. It is used to sidestep or postpone dealing with issues or to withdraw from a threatening situation. It is helpful when people need to cool down before addressing a conflict. It can also be useful to buy time to further analyze a conflict. When one senses that the presenting conflict may only be a symptom of a deeper one, temporary avoidance can give a person the time necessary to determine what the conflict is and how to appropriately address it. Likewise, it is useful when someone needs to gather more information before making a decision. When actors or circumstances are in flux, avoiding behavior sometimes results in resolution because the people in conflict leave or the issues change. However, if conditions remain the same, the conflict is likely to resurface.

Compromising behavior: a style in which people exchange concessions on less important issues to gain agreement on their most important ones. It is common when people are negotiating about some resource. It is particularly helpful in developing temporary settlements or in arriving at expedient decisions under the pressure of time. Because its outcome leaves all parties partially dissatisfied, it often serves as a fallback method of conflict resolution when collaborating or competing methods have been attempted but have not worked.

Collaborating behavior: a style in which a person tries to work with other people to satisfy the key concerns of all involved. It is useful when the issues in the conflict are too important to each side to be compromised. It requires a degree of trust so that people can explore each other's underlying concerns and creatively consider ways to address them. A means to innovative solutions, collaboration is effective when people must maintain positive relationships after the conflict is resolved.

A board chair, by his or her own demeanor, can model the type of conflict behavior he or she would like to instill in the culture of the board. This takes work and time, but it is an important form of leadership for a chair and a valuable legacy to leave to an organization's future leadership.

How Culture and Communication Influence Conflict

Not only are we products of individual temperament, unique life experience, family upbringing, and established mental patterns, we are also products of the culture in which we live or have lived. Culture establishes many of our communication patterns as well as our basic values — and often these are so familiar that they are invisible to us. When not understood, these cultural patterns can be a source of conflict, particularly in the nonprofit organization staffed and governed by people from a variety of cultures. An understanding of cultural differences can be the key to conflict resolution.

The Role of Communication Style in Conflict

Another important element that influences conflict is communication style, both verbal and nonverbal. While individuals from the same culture often have different *personal* communication styles, they still share many culturally specific patterns of communication. Language is one such shared pattern. Even so, misunderstandings about the meaning of words are a big source of conflict, even among people who share the same language.

Though our choice of words can sometimes avert or create conflict, language is only one means by which we communicate. Experts estimate that 60 to 90 percent of communication occurs through means *other than* words. Intonation, smiles and laughter, speaking pace, gestures, posture, eye contact, and physical distance all have culturally specific meanings. With the exception of several universal facial gestures like a smile of happiness, a face fallen in sadness, or a look of disgust, most gestures are culturally bound. Even the universal sign of happiness, a smile, can be used to hide disagreement or embarrassment in some cultures. A gesture or expression that one culture views as positive, another may view as negative. Needless to say, it is easy to misinterpret nonverbal communication, particularly if we assume that other people's nonverbal cues have the same meaning as ours.

When Words and Gestures Don't Match

Even when all parties in a conflict are from the same culture, gestures can overpower words. A dramatic example of this is the story of the board of a health-related organization. Its board was making some difficult decisions about the future of the organization. Emotions were high and people had strong convictions about what they wanted the organization to become. One board member had the habit of smiling almost all the time. Even in the course of heated debate, he delivered his statements with a smile. He often said highly critical things about the staff and other board members, all through a big toothy grin. Because his nonverbal message contradicted his words, he caused a great deal of confusion among the people listening to him. Reactions of other board members and staff grew intense. They responded with anger and viewed the smiling board member as untrustworthy. He lost all his credibility with the board and staff because of his body language.

How to Manage Conflict

A Step-By-Step Process for Managing Conflicts

Following is a recommended series of steps for a typical conflict resolution process. It is written as a guideline, and a conflict manager may want to modify it, depending on the circumstances and people involved. It is written to the person who is designing and taking leadership as the key facilitator in a conflict resolution process. In the case of conflicts on boards, this is most often the board chair, with the support of the chief executive. Both the chair and the chief executive will find it helpful to be familiar with the process because in most cases they will be working together to analyze the conflict, design the process, and see the conflict to its resolution.

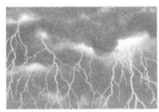

1. Identify the conflict

Learn to watch for signs of serious conflict. Watch for changes in communication, recurring tensions, or other patterns.

2. Decide whether to intervene

Decide whether to intervene in the conflict and consider the possible consequences of intervening or not intervening.

3. Identify parties, issues, and emotions

Collect as much information about the conflict as possible, gathering each person's perspective on the issue.

4. Analyze the conflict

Take time to formally analyze the conflict on the basis of the information gathered.

5. Design the process

Plan the way to bring the parties together to address the conflict.

6. Educate parties and get agreement to participate

Explain everything that will happen in the conflict resolution process and ask each person to agree to participate.

7. Conduct the process

Hold one or more meetings to help the parties find a creative solution to their differences.

8. Celebrate and check in

Celebrate the end of the conflict. Then set up a system to ensure that the agreement is followed and the parties remain satisfied.

Step 1: Identify the Conflict

As a board chair or chief executive, it is wise to be alert to behaviors and interactions that may signal a conflict, either between the two organizational leaders or among board members. Though it's important to keep an eye open for signs of conflict, most times conflicts will find you. Still, there is a much greater benefit to finding trouble *before* it finds you. Usually conflicts identified early are easier to resolve because they have not escalated to a high level of emotional intensity or complexity. By the time people are uncomfortable enough to bring a conflict to your attention, it has likely been brewing for some time. People will have invested a great deal of emotion, thought, and energy in the conflict. If, as the board chair, you or your chief executive notes tension or misunderstandings between board members, take the initiative to check it out. A quick telephone conversation or a chat over lunch can go a long way to clarify issues or reestablish positive relationships. The same interpersonal skills that enabled you to gain your position of leadership can help now. These quick interventions are an essential part of the chair's job, and they may help offset the larger conflicts for which the more formal step-by-step approach is designed.

Pay attention to subtle clues to take note of possible conflicts brewing. As difficult as it is to find time in your busy schedule, make some time

Resolving Your Own Conflict

Most of this book focuses on how nonprofit leaders can help others in conflict. But no one is free from conflict. Inevitably conflict will sometimes directly involve the leaders themselves.

All the concepts and skills offered in this book can help a person when he or she is part of a conflict, but they are much more difficult to apply to yourself than to others. Like anyone in conflict, your emotions, assumptions, and personal goals will hinder your objectivity. It will help to know your own physical and emotional responses to conflict, and use whatever works to calm yourself in order to think as objectively as possible.

Find time to analyze the conflict, using the steps provided in this book. Keep in mind that you can't be as impartial about your own conflicts as you can about those of others. If the conflict is one you can handle directly with the person involved, then do so. This will not only likely resolve the conflict, but will also set a tone in the organization for others to do the same. The following are most important tips when you work to resolve a conflict of your own:

- Keep calm and clear-headed, and don't get hooked into responding to other people's emotional tenor.
- Actively gather information about the situation and be open to clarifying and changing your own assumptions about the conflict and potential solutions.
- Be clear about your own and your organization's interests and open to valuing the interests of others in the conflict.
- Remember that both substantive issues and relationships need to be attended to in conflicts among people who will relate to one another in the future.

to simply focus on the people at the board table. Watch your board members, listen to them, and get a feel for their tone, demeanor, and body language. Do this during a meeting, over lunch, or at a coffee break or board social event; *it is more a matter of focus than of actually performing a new activity.* Look for changes in behavior or patterns of communication. Because conflict is uncomfortable for most people, you will see them reacting to one another differently when they are in conflict. Here are some cues to look for:

Silence. A drop in the amount of communication can often be a signal that something is going on. Conflict is one possibility.

Eye contact. Watch for a change in how people make eye contact. People of European heritage will often avoid eye contact with an individual with whom they are in conflict. (As this is a culturally specific behavior, be aware of cultural differences when interpreting eye contact.)

Humor. Note changes in the level of humor and laughter in interactions. Note whether the nature of the humor changes, particularly if it becomes sarcastic or cynical. Remember that laughter can be a sign of discomfort as well as pleasure.

Word choice. Listen for euphemisms for conflict. Listen for epithets that indicate alienation of individuals in the group.

Tone of voice. Pay attention to intonation as words are spoken — particularly changes that might indicate that conflict is occurring. Please remember that intonation is influenced both by culture and gender.

Body language. Watch how people position their bodies during interactions. Remember that some body language is culturally specific. However, the activity of *mirroring* positions and movements (matching another person's gestures) is shared as a signal of harmony in almost all cultures.

Change in social patterns. Be aware if social patterns change noticeably — for example, a change in who goes to lunch or social events together, or in who is included or excluded in alliances on board issues can indicate conflict.

Style differences. Look for significant differences among individuals in their work and decision-making styles. Unless staff and board members have learned to recognize and value different styles, these can be a common sign — or source — of conflict.

Recurring problems. Recurring troubles between specific individuals or groups may indicate system-induced conflicts.

Cross-program tensions. Watch for recurring tensions between programs or administrative parts of the organization. Some tensions are built into organizational systems as checks and balances, but some go beyond the check and balance purpose and become dysfunctional. The tensions may be the unintentional result of an outmoded organizational policy or procedure.

By putting your attention and skills to work, you may have identified a conflict. Now you have to decide what to do about it.

If you feel you cannot be truly open-minded about the people or issues involved in the dispute, have others handle it.

Step 2: Decide Whether to Intervene

If you think intervention in a particular conflict is needed, consider the following questions.

1. Are you the most appropriate person to help resolve this conflict?

An organization's board of directors is its last resort for internal conflict resolution. However, boards are often untrained in conflict management and are frequently averse to conflict. When a conflict comes to a board for resolution, there is frequently a sense that management did not handle the conflict well (even though this may not be true). There is also a potential for uninformed board members to take sides between staff members, creating a new conflict at the board level. Though the general rule is to handle conflicts as far down on the organizational ladder as possible, conflict between managers or between supervisors and their employees may need executive intervention. Unique circumstances may require the board to handle conflicts throughout the organization.

A conflict that comes to the board can be handled by the board chair or, depending on the circumstances, by the chair of the board's personnel committee or executive committee. In all cases, you as chair will need to assess whether the persons in these positions have the skills to manage the con-

flict, whether they can be objective, and whether they will invest the necessary time. If you are lucky enough to have people who have these characteristics, you may want to consider having them manage the conflict through their subcommittee before it comes to the full board.

Once you have decided if you are the most appropriate person to help resolve the conflict, you can begin to answer question 2.

2. Can you (or whoever you identify) be objective about the people and issues?

All people have opinions and feelings about the people with whom they interact. If you, as board chair, have strong feelings or preferences about any of the parties in a dispute, it will be difficult for you to be objective. In the midst of the process, it will be nearly impossible to mask your personal preferences about people. If these preferences are known, you won't be viewed as neutral by any of the parties. Be brutally honest with yourself. In regard to the parties in the conflict, *you must be able to wholeheartedly say to yourself that you can be objective and impartial.* If you find objectivity a challenge, seek another person to help you manage this conflict.

In regard to the issues, however, you are not truly neutral. You are an advocate for the well-being of the organization you lead. This does not mean you propose your preferred solution to the conflict or adhere blindly to the status quo, but if a proposed solution is bad for the organization (for example, if it breaks the law or an important existing policy, jeopardizes the organization's financial health or reputation, or sets a precedent that will create problems), you should help the disputants find solutions that work for them *and* the organization.

The bottom line is this: If you feel you cannot be truly open-minded about the people or issues involved in the dispute, have others handle it.

3. What are the likely consequences of *not* resolving this issue at this point?

Think through the consequences of entering into or breaking off a conflict resolution process. What will be the best possible outcome if this conflict is not resolved at this point? What are the other possible outcomes? These key questions have two uses in assessing a conflict. First, thinking through the best- and worst-case outcomes for the people involved and your organization helps you clarify how important it is to intervene and what the consequences of not doing so might be. Second, once you have determined your best- and worst-case scenarios, you can decide whether the time is right to intervene and whether you are willing to commit the required time and energy.

4. Can you make the time to deal with the resolution process?

Conflict resolution takes time because it is predominantly a communication process. It clarifies the shortcuts in communication that often contribute to misunderstandings and conflicts. It takes time to gather information about the situation, tailor a process, brief parties about the process, and conduct the conflict resolution discussions. Once you begin, you have to be prepared to efficiently but sensitively carry the process to its end. Of course time varies based on the people and issues, but the time investment for an average conflict is listed in the accompanying box:

Typical Time for Conflict Resolution	
Gather information from involved parties:	45 - 60 minutes for each person
Analyze the conflict and tailor the process:	30 - 60 minutes
Brief parties about the process:	30 - 45 minutes each
Conduct conflict resolution meeting(s):	60 - 120 minutes each

As you can see, the preliminary work you do to gather information, analyze the conflict, tailor the process, and prepare parties for the conflict resolution meeting can take longer than the meeting itself. However, the preliminary work improves the chances for successful conflict resolution.

Many conflicts are resolved in meetings of two hours or less. In cases with multiple issues, many parties, or extremely strong emotions, additional meetings may be needed. However, you can use the chart above to estimate roughly how much time the process will take.

Once you have decided that you should intervene in the conflict, it is time to better understand the conflict you're faced with.

Step 3: Identify Parties, Issues, and Emotions

To understand a conflict well enough to determine how to facilitate a resolution process, you need information. Start with the people who have identified themselves or whom you have identified as the parties in conflict. (It's not uncommon to find additional parties to a conflict as you talk with the identified parties.)

Following are questions you'll need to answer as you identify the people, issues, and emotions in the conflict.

1. Who has a stake in the conflict? These are the parties.

2. Do certain groups have the same interests and positions? Think of like-minded groups as one party when you analyze the conflict.

3. How does each person see the issues (substantive, procedural, relationship, and identity) in the conflict? These are their positions and interests. Mentally note the assumptions or motives each person ascribes to others.

4. What does each party seek as a solution to the conflict? These are their positions.

5. How emotional are people regarding the conflict? Be aware of people's feelings.

Your first step in collecting information is simply to make note of the known parties and make appointments with them to collect information about who is involved, the issues at hand, and their feelings about the situation. As you meet with the parties, the names of other individuals may also crop up. Add these to the list of people to contact. On a board, it is likely that parties are evident and as chair you already know a great deal about them.

However, move cautiously so that you don't make false assumptions about people and their issues.

After you speak with each person, jot down the key answers to the five preceding questions. You do not need extensive notes, just something to jog your memory of the conversation when you analyze the situation. (Keep these notes in a secure place. Dispose of them after the conflict resolution process is complete.)

You may not need to ask for much information about the conflict to get answers to your questions. People are often so relieved to have someone who will listen to their side of the conflict that they are forthcoming. As a result, they will tell you a great deal without your asking specific questions. However, information gathering is an art. You will receive a lot of information at once, and you must sort out the underlying issues and the emotional content that surrounds them.

UNDERLYING ISSUES

People frequently describe a conflict in terms of the absence of the solution they would like to see. They are also likely to describe the other party as somehow blocking that solution. In such cases, ask them to describe the parts of the problem their solution addresses. This can elicit information about people's underlying concerns or needs.

For example, a statement often heard in nonprofit organizations is "If we had the funding, we would offer this needed service." Lack of funding is stated as the problem. Too little money is largely an ongoing condition in nonprofit organizations. Increased funding is only one solution to the problem of wanting to set up a new service that requires resources. There are other solutions, but to figure them out the underlying needs and concerns that the stated solution of funding really addresses must be explored. If staff time is the underlying need that funding will meet, then additional staff, volunteers, interns, or staff reassignments are all alternative solutions to the problem.

The exploration of what needs or concerns a proposed solution (called a *position*) addresses is called *uncovering the interests*. Interests are "the underlying needs or compelling issues of each party in a dispute." Interests often go unstated. The key interests are the essential needs and concerns that a mutually acceptable resolution must address. Understanding them is a critical part of designing a process and crafting a resolution. Sometimes it is easier for a conflict manager to recognize an interest than it is for the party holding the interest because they are so invested in their position.

Many times people become so attached to their solutions that they lose sight of their own basic interests. Helping people articulate and understand their own interests is an important service that a conflict manager offers. As part of the process of understanding positions and interests, a manager can frame the issue in a new way.

Uncovering interests is simple. You must learn the reasons *why* a person takes a particular position or suggests a particular solution. When someone in conflict proposes a solution or position, ask him or her to clarify why a particular solution works. The way you get to *why* is important. A direct *why* can make people feel that you doubt their reasoning, which can make them defensive. Avoid a tone of voice or phrasing that sounds interrogating. Rather, approach the question in a conversational manner. Sometimes you can state, as a guess, what you think a party's interest might be and check it out with them. If you guessed right, great. If you guessed wrong, he or she will correct you. You both win either way. Another benefit of this approach is that when parties say or hear their interests articulated, they feel understood. The parties also discover what elements a resolution must contain to satisfy them.

EMOTIONAL CONTENT

As you uncover the issues and interests in a conflict, you will also encounter the emotions that surround them. Many people have strong feelings when they are engaged in a conflict; adults often experience a conflict with the same emotional intensity they felt as children. People may describe their feelings as they talk with you, but you are even more likely to sense their feelings through their facial expressions, intonation, and body language. They will express — and you will observe — anger, hurt, sadness, guilt, defensiveness, and many other feelings. It is important to acknowledge these feelings, but you must remember that you are not responsible for changing their feelings. However, your recognition of an individual's feelings will usually lower the intensity of the emotion. Lowering the intensity of feelings actually enables people to think more clearly and creatively, because they can better engage the portion of their brain that is muted when emotions are high.

When you acknowledge feelings, use a question or a gentle observation. Never tell people what you think they do or should feel. Whatever you say, be sincere; it is better not to say anything than to use "canned" statements like, "What I think I hear you saying is_____ . " Such phrases are overused and feel manipulative to the person who hears them. Use only affirming comments that feel natural and sincere to you. This makes them believable. Examples of possible responses are

- "You seem upset about that."
- "Does _____ make you angry?" (Use when you think you see nonverbal signs of anger.)
- "Are you worried about _____?"
- "So when that happened, you felt _____?"

Offering affirming comments in the form of questions enables the party to either confirm or correct what you think they may be feeling.

Many of us shy away from talking about feelings when we think another person is emotional. We worry that talking about feelings will unleash a flood of emotion that neither we nor they can handle. This rarely happens, but when it does, it often relieves the pressure and helps the person better manage his or her emotions. More commonly, identifying feelings generally has the effect of lowering people's levels of emotion. Naming emotions also conveys empathy.

If someone's emotions do overwhelm him or her, be patient and wait it out. Offer time, company, or privacy, as the person wishes. The strong emotions will pass, and the pressure of restraining pent-up emotions will be relieved. Then the person will be able to discuss the issue in a more lucid manner.

Step 4: Analyze the Conflict

Your analytic abilities, managerial judgment, and creative thinking are your best tools for analyzing a conflict. You'll screen for problems such as harassment, maltreatment, or illegal behavior, which should be dealt with using processes other than this one. You'll sort the people you've identified into parties and try to understand what their positions are. You'll discover if you need to gather more information before proceeding. You will apply all of these tools to the information you gathered to chart a course to help people resolve their conflict.

Your analysis will answer the following questions:

1. Can this conflict be handled by this informal process?

The first step is to screen the conflict to decide whether it requires a conflict resolution process different from the one described. Such situations include

- harassment,
- discrimination,
- the involvement of vulnerable adults or children,
- evidence of illegal behavior, and
- actions covered under union grievance procedures.

All of these situations require special processes that may make them inappropriate for the informal conflict management process suggested in this book. If you find these situations as you gather information, you will need to follow the particular processes designed for them. The first step is to review your organization's personnel policies. If your nonprofit is unionized, reviewing the contract and grievance procedures is your next step. This is where a chief executive can be of support to the board chair, as he or she will have access to and know the specific policies and procedures that are in practice in the organization.

2. Who are *all* the people with stakes in this conflict?

In Step 3, you identified the people, the parties, their issues, and the emotions surrounding the conflict. Now revisit the list to be sure you know the name of every person who is substantively affecting or being affected by the conflict. These are the people to involve in the conflict management process. You may discover more (or different) parties than originally expected. If you find new parties in the middle of the process, they need to be brought into the discussion — and that means backing up the process a bit so the new parties can catch up.

In addition to the people who are parties to the conflict, there are others who may be directly affected by or concerned about the ultimate resolution. List these people and your supposition about their potential interests. Though these people probably won't be included in the conflict resolution meetings, you may need to ask for their advice or opinions as options are being devised.

3. Are these individuals capable of making rational, informed decisions?

After you have named all the individuals, you need to decide whether they are competent to participate in a conflict resolution process. Most people are. For example, a person who seems overwrought with emotion is still capable of participating; a person who seems overwrought with emotion and is acting out violently is not.

Nonprofits that work with mentally handicapped individuals or other vulnerable people may need to follow a different or modified process when a conflict affects them. In situations involving people who are mentally handicapped, one solution is to have a trusted and competent adviser work with the party throughout the process. If you determine that even with such help the person cannot participate in the process, you might consider whether a proxy might work (with the person's or their guardian's permission). A proxy is a person whose role is much like that of an international diplomat. When conducted with a proxy, the conflict resolution process works a lot like shuttle diplomacy. It entails a lot of conferring and clear communications between the proxy and the party. The proxy may or may not be empowered to make decisions on behalf of the individual he or she represents. This needs to be decided before the conflict resolution process begins. If none of these options are viable, then it may be unwise to continue an informal conflict management process.

4. What are the power relationships among the individuals?

Having identified the parties and decided that they are competent to participate, analyze the power relationships among them. Consider two things about power: determine who has what sorts of power, and who accedes (or does not accede) to that power. Think about how the parties have used their power in the conflict thus far. When one party's use of power is perceived as forcing or blocking, it often creates relationship issues where none existed.

There are several types of power. Formal power is the authority is given by virtue of one's position in society or in an organization. Informal power exists by virtue of a person's personal quali-

ties or relationships with others. These two larger categories of power can be further classified into sanction power, procedural power, referent power, the power of expertise or information, moral power, charismatic power, the power of habit, and nuisance power. Both formal and informal power are equally important to consider when analyzing a conflict and developing a resolution process.

Understanding each party's interests gives you a picture of the content of the conflict and may even show you possibilities for resolution.

5. What gender or cultural differences must be considered?

Consider how culture and gender influence communications and activities in the workplace. Might culture, gender, or other communication differences have created misunderstandings? Are there misunderstandings based on stereotypes regarding culture or gender?

6. How does each person describe the overall conflict?

Use this information to assess how the parties place blame or claim responsibility in the conflict. Consider how readily the parties might agree to participate in a conflict resolution process.

7. What are each party's positions? (What solutions do they seek?)

A party's position is often the solution they propose to resolve the conflict — usually, a solution that addresses their interests only. Note that when stating their overview of the conflict, parties often state their positions as the *lack* of something. You may also note that they describe other parties as blocking their solutions.

8. What does each party say — or what can be inferred — about their key needs and concerns?

Understanding each party's interests gives you a picture of the content of the conflict and may even show you possibilities for resolution. You may have to infer a party's interests from what they have told you in your information-gathering conversations. If you have done this, it will be essential in the conflict management meetings to check whether your inferences are correct. But for the purpose of analyzing a conflict, you can start with educated guesses regarding a party's interests. Be sure to make note of which interests the party identified and which you inferred.

9. What assumptions are people making about one another?

The assumptions people make when in conflict with others is frequently a product of cognitive dissonance, our mental practice of filling in the blanks or changing our perceptions when new information does not jibe with our current understanding of events. Understanding these assumptions will give you important clues about issues that need to be discussed at the conflict resolution meeting. The ultimate goal is for all parties to have the same information. This significantly increases the likelihood of a resolution. Because parties in conflict make many negative assumptions about one another, dispelling inaccurate assumptions is a major contribution to mending relationships. However, in the analysis phase, noting these assumptions is all you need to do.

10. Do some individuals share interests and positions?

Initially, you gathered information about the people, their positions and interests, their emotions, and their level of power. Now is the time to group these individuals into parties. Make rough groupings based on the similarities in their interests and positions. You may need to adjust these groupings as you further analyze the various interests of the people involved. People with similar positions, even if their interests differ, are likely to view one another as allies. When they discover that their interests differ, they may dissolve their alliance.

11. Are people's interests substantive, procedural, relationship-based, or identity-based? Which of these is the primary concern?

As each party's interests and positions come to light, it is helpful to consider whether they are about relationships among people, substantive matters (resources or time), processes and procedures (how decisions are made or how systems work), or

As much as you care about the individuals on your board and involved in your nonprofit, your first responsibility is to the organization you lead.

strongly held beliefs or practices that are part of their identity. Most conflicts contain more than one of these types of interests, but it is helpful to sort them out when possible. Knowing the types of interests underlying the conflict will help you think about the goals of the process you will design in subsequent steps. Finally, you may note which interests seem to be most important to the parties. These are likely the key matters that must be addressed to get a mutually satisfactory resolution.

12. Is the conflict interpersonal or is it induced by the system — or is it both?

Sorting out whether a conflict is interpersonal or system-induced is challenging because conflicts initially created by organizational systems frequently become interpersonal. Consider whether procedures, policies, or practices in the organization are unnecessarily fostering conflict. Be aware that some systems that create conflict in organizations are necessary: They are designed as checks and balances that preserve accountability and distribute power. Other system-induced conflicts are vestiges of policies, procedures, or decisions that are outdated. As organizations grow and change, ways of working and communicating also need to change. Yet many become traditional, whether or not they fit the current organization and its staff. As you analyze a conflict, be alert to system-induced conflicts and be open-minded about changing the organizational systems that create them. Such conflicts may lead to positive changes in your organization's policies or procedures.

13. Are there known limitations to potential resolutions that you must impose on behalf of the organization?

You may find that some potential solutions to conflict are limited by finances, policies, mission goals, ethical standards, union procedures, or legal requirements.

For example, a nonprofit neighborhood day care center wrestled with a conflict between its mission and a potential new funding source. A contribution from a huge corporation to an umbrella agency made new grants possible that would help the day care center meet rigorous accreditation standards and improve its quality. The center applied for and received a grant. The grant contract was sent to the board president for his signature. Upon reading the contract, the president noted that if the center accepted the grant, employees of the funding corporation would, in perpetuity, receive priority for their children to attend the day care center. This was against the mission of the organization, which was established to serve an economically and racially diverse clientele from the neighborhood. Accepting the grant would require the center to serve the children of the corporation before those of the neighborhood.

The board was in conflict over whether to accept the much-needed money. It had to weigh whether its mission of service to the neighborhood was more important than the financial support, which would improve its quality. The board members were all parents whose children were already enrolled in the day care center and who would directly benefit from the improvements the grant offered. The board resolved the conflict by declining the grant, and the people most concerned about maintaining the focus on diversity and neighborhood agreed to head an alternative fund-raising effort to pay for accreditation and improved quality.

Be aware of these types of limitations prior to a conflict resolution meeting and help the parties understand the constraints during their proposal of solutions. First be sure that the organization's limits are indeed nonnegotiable. Then be prepared to explain why the limits are necessary for the sake of the organization. You will probably not use this information immediately, but it is wise to have thought it through during the conflict analysis — *before* embarking on the conflict management process.

It is common to want to solve a conflict as rapidly as possible. It is easy, and generally a mistake, to dive into helping resolve a conflict without thinking through the preceding questions. This kind of formal analysis is not natural for most of us. Taking the time to analyze the conflict can save a great deal of time and many missteps as you manage the conflict resolution process.

Step 5: Design the Process

You can now design the conflict resolution process. It is possible that after you've concluded your analysis of the conflict in Step 4, you'll realize that you are not the best person to manage this particular conflict. Relax — all is not lost! Review the material in Step 2: Decide Whether to Intervene. Keep these thoughts in mind as you mull over possible candidates for the job:

- The person must have conflict management skills.

- All parties must view the person as impartial.

- You will need to talk with the person about the information you have gathered — you can't just turn over your notes to him or her.

- The person will need to be the one to design the process, with your advice.

- You will need to tell the person of any restrictions to possible solutions you identified in your analysis.

- The person will need to check back with you if proposed solutions have implications for other organizational policies and procedures.

- You will need to inform the parties with whom you spoke during the information-gathering phase. They will probably want to know why you have selected this person as conflict manager, that the person has your confidence, and what strengths he or she will bring to the process. The new conflict manager may want to meet briefly with each party to develop rapport.

- Most importantly, the person you select as conflict manager needs to know that he or she has your backing, support, and trust.

An external mediator will have his or her own ideas about process. Be sure to select a mediator who is flexible and sensitive to your organization's culture and whom you judge all involved can work with effectively. This decision is one you and the chief executive may want to make jointly.

Answering the following questions will help you decide who should best handle the conflict.

1. What are the goals of the process?

Obviously, the goal is to end the conflict. But there is more to it than that. Conflicts may require additional goals:

■ If the people involved must work together regularly, an important goal will be to reestablish trust and harmony — to restore the relationship.

This is true for conflicts between individual board members or among staff. If the relationship is not mended, you will find new conflicts rekindling left and right. This situation calls for a relationship goal.

■ If the conflict is with a vendor who you will likely quit using and with whom a lawsuit would be costly, resolving the substantive interests is

Ways to Balance Power

Before

■ If the less powerful party fears retribution from the more powerful party, choose a conflict manager with authority over the more powerful party and who knows the issues. People generally try to behave reasonably and fairly in the presence of someone who has authority over them.

■ If you have authority over the more powerful party, that is a strong reason for you to be the conflict manager.

■ Review the section on different types of power. (See page 25) Consider the powers each party has available and how these might be used to level the playing field.

■ Help the less powerful party understand the different types of power available to them, such as the powers of expertise, association, and information.

■ Ensure that both parties have access to the same information regarding matters being discussed.

■ Encourage the less powerful party to get help understanding the information if it is new to him or her. Don't coach the person yourself, however, or you will jeopardize your impartiality.

■ Encourage both parties to prepare thoroughly for the meetings, including rehearsing what they will say with a friend or colleague.

■ Help the parties explore assumptions they may hold about their options and choices.

■ Help both parties determine the best-case and worst-case scenarios.

During

■ Encourage the less powerful party to be assertive in expressing ideas and feelings.

■ Let the less powerful party express his or her perspective first.

■ Provide equal time for each party to speak, limiting interruptions, stopping inappropriate language or behavior quickly, and directing parties to frame their presentations in terms of their own experiences and feelings (as opposed to blaming or speaking for the other party).

■ To constrain the more powerful party, suggest that he or she communicate in a way that does not intimidate the less powerful party.

■ When appropriate, reframe the issues on a shared, higher level in which each party has an equal stake.

After

■ To reduce the possibility of retribution, be sure that the agreement includes some form of monitoring and evaluation of the more powerful party's behavior.

To maintain trust, you must employ power-balancing techniques subtly, using them primarily with individual parties and not in the presence of others. Efforts at balancing power are readily perceived as taking sides, which will greatly diminish your effectiveness as a conflict manager. Power imbalances should be considered when designing a conflict management process, during the conflict resolution process itself, and as resolutions are developed. Because power ebbs and flows among parties throughout a conflict management process, you will need to remain continually observant of power.

much more important than resolving the relationship issues. This situation calls for a substantive goal.

■ If the conflict is between management and employees or management and the board, the goal might include changing or clarifying processes in the organization along with rebuilding damaged relationships. Here procedural interests are foremost, coupled with relationship interests when staff and board will continue to work together. This situation calls for a procedural goal.

Identifying the key goals of the process will help you decide how much effort and time to invest on certain issues, which in turn is likely to shape the way you facilitate conflict management meetings. As you design the conflict resolution process, take a moment to state the goals for relationship, substantive, procedural, and other issues. Look over the most important interests in your notes from the conflict analysis steps. Note the types of interests marked as key to the parties (substantive, procedural, relationship-based, or identity-based). These will point to the goals. Consider whether you think this conflict takes a classic shape. If it is shaped like a spiral or subtle conflict, anticipate that unidentified interests are likely to arise in the resolution process. Think about the future activities of the people involved in the conflict, because expectations of future interactions definitely influence goals. It is useful to think this through in advance, but don't be surprised if things change as you get new information in the conflict resolution meeting. Having a process in mind gives you and the parties the confidence to undertake the conflict resolution, but flexibility is critical to its success.

2. How much time will the process take?

Now that you have spoken with all the parties, you can estimate time for this particular conflict. To develop an estimate, consider the number of people involved, the quantity and complexity of issues, how close the parties are in their positions and interests, and how damaged relationships are. The conflict manager and the parties will find an estimate useful for planning their own work. Just re-

> *Any time you can get people in conflict to work together or agree — even about the weather — you are reinforcing their ability to work through a conflict together.*

mind everyone to be flexible — conflict resolution is a process with twists, turns, and surprises!

Used judiciously, time limitations can encourage people to settle disputes. While people need and want time to air their side of a dispute, often a deadline helps them stay focused and decide what is truly important to them. Time running out or the possibility of having to devote another meeting to the issue helps people sort out their issues and come to a conclusion. Like many conflict resolution techniques, deadlines must be used like a spice — just a little, and at the right moment.

Sometimes having a set time limit in mind helps people feel good about resolving an issue sooner than anticipated — it sets everyone up as working together to beat the clock. Any time you can get people in conflict to work together or agree — even about the weather — you are reinforcing their ability to work through a conflict together.

3. How will power imbalances be handled?

Because organizations are generally hierarchical, people have different degrees of authority and power over others. Most people view such power as the only power in an organization and so find it intimidating to try to resolve conflict with someone they view as more powerful. Often their biggest fear is retribution by the more powerful individual. Fear of retribution frequently keeps people at different levels in the organization from dealing with conflict. You need to deal with this fear up front — usually *before* people agree to try to resolve the conflict.

4. How will you handle people's emotions regarding the conflict?

In Step 3: Identify Parties, Issues, and Emotions, you assessed the intensity of people's emotions. Now it's time to incorporate your assessment into the design of the conflict management process.

As mentioned before, just talking about the conflict with an impartial person often considerably de-escalates emotions. But don't expect a person to remain emotionless at a face-to-face meeting with the other party just because he or she has released emotions in previous discussions with you. Like power, emotions ebb and flow, especially during the early part of a conflict resolution process when people are airing their differences.

The intensity of people's emotions is a clue to the importance of their issues. But don't underestimate the importance of feelings, even if emotions don't seem strong. Many resolutions ultimately hinge on an apology or an acknowledgment of one or both parties' misjudgment of people or events.

The following are guidelines for designing a process that accounts for people's emotional states and fosters a resolution that helps repair wounded feelings:

■ Attend to people's need to manage their emotions by having tissues and water within reach.

■ Seat people who are in conflict so that when they look up they are not forced to make eye contact.

■ Ensure that the meeting room is private so that if people get emotional they don't have to worry that uninvolved people can hear or see them.

■ Make all parties aware that they can call a break or a caucus at any time — for example, when emotions are getting difficult to manage.

■ Call breaks or caucuses yourself if you sense that people are getting quite emotional.

■ Be available to hold caucuses with emotional parties so that they can emote in private with you. (This is a situation in which you will want to empathize, but not sympathize.) Be sure to hold caucuses with all other parties.

■ Tactfully name emotions (understating them somewhat) to help people feel understood and de-escalate emotions.

With agreement from all parties, people can invite someone to attend the meeting to lend emotional support. (Support people should *not* be allowed to participate in the discussions.)

Use your interpersonal knowledge and intuition to judge people's emotions. If you think emotions are so strong that the parties cannot face one another without an emotional outburst, you might design the first phase of the discussion as a form of shuttle diplomacy on your part. Shuttle diplomacy should not replace face-to-face conflict resolution unless cultural norms make cross-gender or face-to-face meetings inadvisable. Seeing the other party,

Confidentiality is most important to the success of a conflict resolution process, and the importance must be stressed with all people involved.

noting their reactions, and hearing their voices as they state their concerns can help people recognize the humanity in the other person, a perspective that is often distorted or missing during a conflict.

5. In what setting will the meetings occur?

The physical setting of a conflict resolution meeting can influence the process more than one would expect. There are several considerations when choosing the setting.

■ The setting should be a private space, free from interruptions by people, telephones, or beepers.

■ The space should not "belong" to either party. There is a psychological advantage to being on one's own turf, so it is best to be in a neutral space. If the conflict manager's office is private and free from interruptions, it gives the facilitator a helpful home court advantage. It is also wise to move people away from the location of their conflict, if possible. This gives the parties a fresh view.

■ The space should be comfortable. It should have comfortable chairs, good lighting, and temperature control. Amenities like coffee, tea, and water make the face-to-face encounter feel a bit less hostile for the parties.

■ A critical consideration is seating arrangements. Use your authority as conflict manager to recommend an arrangement to the parties.

Seating is important for two reasons. First, when people are feeling uncomfortable or anxious about a face-to-face meeting, they often direct their remarks to the facilitator while the other party listens. This often helps people be frank and feel understood. Thus, the seating arrangement should make it easy to see and address the facilitator, especially early in the process.

The second reason for careful seating is related to eye contact in communication. Even when making direct eye contact is culturally acceptable for an individual, it is often uncomfortable when the individual feels strong negative emotions toward another person. Seating people at angles to one another allows them to choose when and whether to make eye contact. As emotions de-escalate, you are likely to see people who normally make eye contact initiate it again. Also, parties will increasingly direct their comments to one another.

Round and square tables work best for this angled arrangement, but if you find you are at a long rectangular table, cluster people at one end and place parties diagonally across from one another. Be sure to position yourself near the parties. If you are at the opposite end of the table, the parties will have a hard time seeing and making eye contact with you. You will seem removed from the process, physically and psychologically. This will reduce your influence over events.

Put the parties at arm's length distance from one another, as this makes physical contact more difficult and eliminates potential intimidation. If it is possible that intimidation could escalate into a physical conflict, arrange to meet in a space where people are nearby in case you have to call for help.

Another option is open seating — such as a living room environment with armchairs or couches. Use this when you are sure people are comfortable with one another. Though more formal, tables offer people some psychological (and physical) protection. They form a barrier by setting a defined distance between people and also give people a place to set papers and rest their arms. Open seating sets a more informal tone and gives a feeling of openness, but it does not offer the protection a table does. Your understanding of the people and the situation will guide you in arranging an appropriate setting.

6. How will you protect people's need for privacy and confidentiality?

Confidentiality is most important to the success of a conflict resolution process, and its importance must be stressed with all people involved. What is said in meetings, as well as the observations and opinions about what occurred in meetings, must be held in confidence by everyone. (This means not even telling significant others or dearest friends.) The reason is simple. When people face someone with whom they have a conflict, they feel vulnerable about what may occur within the meeting. They also fear something they say or do will be represented to others in ways that will belittle or harm them. In order for parties to feel they can be both honest and direct in a conflict resolution setting, they must feel that what is said will remain private among the people involved in the process. As mentioned previously, confidentiality may not apply if

issues of harassment, maltreatment, or certain illegalities are involved. With the guidance of the chief executive, it is the chair's responsibility to take alternative action, and it is not appropriate to handle such issues using this conflict resolution process.

In many mediations, mediators have people sign an agreement stating that what is said in the mediation will remain entirely confidential unless all parties jointly agree to release the information. If your situation warrants this formality, you can request this. The agreement includes a statement about confidentiality. Most times, having people agree orally in each other's presence at the first meeting is enough. Remind all parties about this agreement at the end of the process.

The chair and others involved may choose to take notes during meetings to help them remember what was said or to remind them of things they want to ask or say. These notes should either be destroyed or kept by the facilitator (not the participants) after each meeting. When the conflict resolution process has ended, the notes should be destroyed. Similarly, flip charts or erasable boards used during meetings should be destroyed or erased.

When public information is part of the discussion and is easily accessible through other sources, it does *not* become confidential simply because of the conflict resolution process. For example, if the organization's budget is discussed in a conflict resolution meeting and it is a readily available document, it is not confidential. However, what people had to say about the budget — their opinions and concerns about it — is private and confidential. So are observations of the participants' emotional states during that discussion. Personal matters, feelings, opinions, and the overall content of a conflict resolution meeting must be confidential. If there is any doubt about the public nature of information, it is wise to ask the participants if they have any concerns about the information being discussed outside of the conflict resolution process. If someone does have concerns, it is wisest to consider the information confidential.

Because this is an informal, cooperative process, no formal sanctions are built in for someone who breaks confidentiality. However, the process is embedded in an organization that has sanction power. A party that breaks confidentiality risks the disapproval of the organization's leaders, loss of credibility, and subsequent loss of power. The breach could have long-term effects on opportunities for advancement and other organizational rewards and benefits. The knowledge of potential sanctions will deter most employees from breaching confidence.

If a serious breach occurs, end the conflict resolution process because trust in both the process and the other parties will have eroded. However, check with the parties before unilaterally ending the process. Shuttle diplomacy might be a backup approach, if parties agree, although neither relationship nor identity conflicts are well served by shuttle diplomacy. If this option is not feasible, it is likely that more formal processes will be needed. At this point call your attorney for advice about how to proceed.

Step 6: Determine Who to Consult

If you determine that the conflict is related to a system in your organization, you should have the chief executive consult with an employee who oversees the system. You may want to involve this person in one or more conflict resolution meetings if the parties agree. Or you might consult with them and bring the information to the discussions. If the person joins the conflict resolution meeting, he or she also must agree to confidentiality.

Step 7: Educate Parties and Get Agreement to Participate

There's no sense trying to resolve a conflict if the parties won't participate. In this step, you meet with the parties individually, tell them how the process will work, and ask them to agree to participate. Your motto regarding the conflict resolution process should be "no surprises."

As you meet with each person individually, tell them what to expect from the conflict resolution process — what the process steps are and what your role will be. Discuss it in detail and answer all their questions. Tell them both the positives and the negatives. Assure them that you will work to keep the discussions orderly and constructive. This private one-on-one meeting to explain the process and the ground rules is your opportunity to get people to agree to participate. It is also your chance to coach people, particularly the less powerful party, about how to prepare for and fully participate in the conflict resolution meeting.

A checklist of all the process steps you will want to cover with the parties is on the following page. Use this checklist twice: first when you are educating the parties privately and again at the opening of the first conflict management meeting between the parties. After you have made sure the person understands the process, you can ask him or her to agree to participate.

Process Steps Checklist

When you meet with each person involved in the conflict, you will need to describe how the conflict resolution process works. Also repeat this explanation at the beginning of the conflict resolution meeting between the two parties. People need to hear the rules twice — once in private, so they can express all their doubts, concerns, and questions, and once at the beginning of the meeting. The repetition reminds the participants of the steps they will follow and assures each person that the others have been advised of the same steps and ground rules.

❑   1. The conflict resolution meeting will open with the conflict manager welcoming people, introducing them if necessary.

❑   2. The group will discuss comfort issues and logistics, including location of bathrooms, refreshments, seating, time limitations, and dates for future meetings.

❑   3. The conflict managers will discuss the process and the ground rules:
- The goal and benefits of the conflict resolution process
- The conflict manager role as impartial facilitator and as the organization's steward
- Expected decorum
- Confidentiality and concept of good faith
- Alternatives to this process
- Use of caucus
- How the meeting will proceed
- The role of outsiders, if any
- Questions about ground rules
- Any additions to ground rules as discussed and agreed to by all parties

❑   4. The parties will make an oral or written agreement to participate in and follow ground rules.

❑   5. The conflict manager will briefly and generally describe the conflict as he or she understands it.

❑   6. Each party will voice his or her understanding of the conflict.

❑   7. The parties and conflict manager will discuss and clarify their understandings of one another's perspectives on the conflict.

❑   8. The parties and conflict manager will identify the key interests and establish an order in which to discuss them.

❑   9. The parties will generate ideas for solutions to key concerns.

❑   10. The parties will evaluate solutions in light of the interests they've identified.

❑   11. The parties will select mutually agreeable solutions.

❑   12. The parties will discuss implementation, monitoring, and follow-up to the solutions.

❑   13. The parties and conflict manager will fine-tune and write up the agreed-upon resolution.

❑   14. The conflict manager will initiate a way to celebrate the resolution.

❑   15. The conflict manager will ensure follow-up.

(continued page 34)

Process Steps Checklist (cont'd)

Sometimes people feel more able to participate in a conflict resolution process if they have the company of someone they trust. For this to happen, *both* parties must agree to the presence of others. Before and during the first meeting, you will need to clarify what role one or more additional people will play and then stick to whatever is decided. Usually the participation of trusted friends or advisers helps the process. However, such participation must be managed with care. If the parties agree to involve outsiders, follow these steps:

❑ 1. Clarify with the party and the party's adviser the exact role the adviser will play. For example, the adviser may be present but be silent during the meeting, offering advice and support in private; they may provide technical information in the meeting or at a caucus; or they may be full participants in the meeting. (Experience suggests not allowing full participation, even though it is an option. Advisers can escalate a conflict if, as they advocate for a friend, they disregard the impact of such advocacy on the future relationship of the parties.)

❑ 2. Be sure both parties agree on outside participation and on the type and amount of participation. Usually, the parties want equal treatment. Shuttle between the parties until you have complete agreement on the rules for adviser participation.

❑ 3. Be sure the advisers understand and agree to follow the rules before the first meeting.

❑ 4. At the first meeting, when all are present, repeat the rules that everyone has agreed the outsiders will follow. Be sure that everyone agrees once again to follow these rules; it is important that everyone witnesses the agreement in person. At this time parties and their advisers may choose to modify some rules. This is fine, as long as everyone at the meeting agrees to the modifications.

On rare occasions someone will object to an outside adviser during the meeting itself. If this happens, end the meeting and meet with the person privately to learn why they have had a change of heart. You will need to address their concerns or change your process.

Step 8: Conduct the Process

Once the parties have agreed to participate, it's time to bring them together to tell their stories, listen to one another, generate possible solutions, and choose a resolution. Though there are many variations in the process, the basic steps are as follows:

1. Set up the meeting environment

Be sure to arrive before the participants so you can set up the meeting room. Whatever setting you choose, arrange it to improve the likelihood of resolution as discussed in Step 5: Design the Process. If by some accident you arrive after parties have seated themselves, start by rearranging people, if needed. As the facilitator you have that authority, so use it.

Have pens, paper, a box of tissues, a flip chart or erasable board, and markers at the ready. Give the participants pens and paper so they can take notes to help them remember points they want to clarify or questions they want to ask. Remind them, though, that their notes are not for documentation and that you will either gather them at the end of each meeting or ask them to destroy them before leaving the room.

2. Open the meeting

When opening the meeting, your job will be to reassure parties, decrease their anxiety, and ensure that everyone knows they are following the same rules. The first step in opening a meeting is to welcome everyone, make necessary introductions, and explain the process steps for the meeting. You will have done this once before in individual meetings with the parties (Step 6). Doing it again has the following benefits:

- Everyone hears the same information at the same time.
- Introductory comments give people time to calm down. Take your time explaining the process steps (See Step 6) and answering questions. This may take up to a half hour.
- You can reassure the participants about your own faith in the process and their abilities to resolve the situation. Say only things you actually believe, but do try to be positive while acknowledging the challenge everyone at the table faces.
- You can build the parties' trust in you by explaining what you have already done as part of the process — information gathering, individual meetings with parties, thinking through the process, and so forth. Be sure to describe these activities in a way that establishes you as fair and evenhanded and does not give any specifics you have learned.
- If appropriate, you can talk about alternatives to settling the dispute. With luck, participants will view the process on which you are about to embark as the most promising.

Next, discuss the basic rules that all conflict resolution meetings follow:

- People must speak respectfully to one another.
- A common way to ensure respectful dialogue is to have people phrase their thoughts from their own perspective. Beginning statements with the pronoun "I" makes accusations, blaming, and belittling difficult. Participants are expected to speak and act in good faith — to tell the truth as they know it and to agree only to actions they are willing to do.
- Everyone involved must keep all the information confidential. If parties want to sign a confidentiality agreement, this is the time to do so.

Find out if the parties want to modify the ground rules. Ask them to discuss and agree on how they will interact in this process. This can give them their first experience in finding common ground, in making an agreement, and in developing hope about their larger dispute.

Next, discuss the meeting mechanics:

- Clarify the roles of people attending the meeting (friends and advisers who are not parties).
- Let everyone know the time the meeting will end.
- Explain that people may ask to take breaks or request caucuses with the facilitator at any time. Remind them what caucuses are and how they work.

3. Have each party describe his or her experience without interruptions.

This is the opportunity for the parties to hear one another's concerns in full in a structured, safe environment. Have one party state his or her understanding of the issues, what is personally important about the issues, and if he or she chooses, his or her feelings about the conflict. Rarely do people need much coaching in this step. They have practiced by

How to Conduct Breaks and Caucuses

Any participant can call a break for comfort purposes, time to think, or when people become weary, distracted, or overcome by emotion. Caucuses are private, confidential meetings between any people involved in the conflict resolution process. Anyone participating in a conflict resolution meeting can call a caucus. During a caucus, the conflict manager meets independently and confidentially with each party for the same amount of time. If this does not occur, the party you did not meet with may doubt your impartiality. Keep caucuses relatively brief, or the waiting party may become anxious.

They can be used when
- the discussion seems repetitive;
- you sense missing information;
- you cannot quite follow the logic or sequence of statements, even after asking for and getting clarification;
- you sense emotions escalating; or
- you think people might need to vent.

In a caucus you can get clarification, test out your ideas and observations, or have one of the parties test out thoughts he or she is hesitant to express at the table. You can role-play the situation or coach the party about how to express his or her ideas. If the party feels unable to speak, you can carry his or her idea to the other party. If the first party does not care to present the information, you may not do so without their express permission. This will break confidentiality and you will lose that person's trust.

When a party uses a caucus to vent during a tense situation, avoid agreeing or disagreeing with the party even as you affirm the party's feelings. Occasionally you can present another perspective as a way to reframe the situation, but do so carefully and sparingly or your reframing will be perceived as partiality.

---

telling the conflict manager many of these things in their private meeting. Once one party has described his or her experience, the other party does the same — also without interruptions.

Parties usually want to interrupt each other to debate points. Recommend that they write down their questions and comments about one another's perspectives while listening, and save them for the next step. This eliminates interruptions and helps each party remember their comments for the next step, in which discussion is encouraged.

4. Invite questions for clarification of different experiences

After each party has given his or her view, both the facilitator and the parties can ask for clarification. This step can be contentious because the parties want to tell each other why they are wrong. The point is to understand one another's perspective, not debate it. However, some debate usually occurs; if it is limited, it is not a problem.

5. Discuss and sort issues

In this step the parties, with your help, try to untangle the web of misunderstanding and disagreement and break it into distinct (but often interrelated) issues. Write the issues on the flip chart or erasable board. Parties may modify or change what you write, which helps them clarify their thoughts. As facilitator you should use your skills in seeking interests, reframing issues, and uncovering the interests embedded in positions. Once all the positions and interests have been identified and listed, you should be prepared to prioritize them. Often this is a good time to suggest a break, noting the progress already made.

6. Decide what issues to discuss first

Depending on the situation, there may be a logical sequence in which to address related issues. Go with what the parties choose. However, it is generally wise to start with an issue that's easy to resolve — either because it is simple or because people have little disagreement about it. Getting even a simple is-

---

sue tentatively settled creates a feeling of optimism and makes tackling harder issues more promising. A flip chart or an erasable board is useful for this step.

7. Discuss issues and generate ideas for solutions within any known limitations

Now we move into the integrative part of the conflict resolution process. Parties begin to discuss single issues in the order they determined and begin to generate possible solutions, each time evaluating whether the solutions address their interests. This step is repeated for each issue. If the parties get stuck on an issue, put that one on hold and move on to the next one. As momentum builds toward resolution, there is often a better chance of successfully resolving the sticky point later. There is no need to finalize the solution for each issue at this point. The group will review all the solutions and how they fit together in the next step.

This is the creative part of the process. To help parties explore potential solutions, you can reframe issues, ask questions, and politely challenge their assumptions.

8. Review and modify the issues and possible solutions

Once the parties have discussed possible solutions for all the issues, they can review them as a whole and modify them as necessary. This is also the time to discuss concerns about implementation or follow-up. Sometimes at this juncture new issues suddenly arise. This happens because an interest was not addressed in a previously devised solution. This is rarely the result of someone being obstreperous or creating a spiral conflict. When people are intensely emotional, the conflict seems like a jumble of issues, and they are not clear about what interests are really important to them. As the integration phase proceeds, people grow more optimistic, more creative, and clearer about what is important to them — and an undiscovered interest suddenly surfaces. Be patient and work on the newly surfaced interest as you did on earlier issues.

9. Agree to a resolution

When all the pieces have come together, the parties agree to a resolution. To be sure everyone has the same understanding of the agreement, the facilitator can draft the resolution and have the parties refine it. Reading an agreed-upon resolution seems to encourage people to be sure they understand the meaning of its language. This can also help prevent future misinterpretations.

10. Formalize the agreement

There are several options for formalizing the agreement. The facilitator can read it and get oral agreement, the parties can finalize it with a handshake, or they can sign a written letter of understanding. Even though the agreement is not a formal document, there are times when people feel more confident when they have an agreement in writing.

> *When people work through a conflict, there is reason to celebrate.*

Step 9: Celebrate

When people work through a conflict, there is reason to celebrate. Given that everyone wants to get back to business, this is an easy step to forget. Don't. View it as an investment in people's willingness and abilities to resolve future conflicts, preferably on their own.

A celebration ends what was likely a difficult set of interactions on a positive note. Base the celebration on the situation and people. It need be no more elaborate than starting a round of thank-yous or handshakes. It usually includes the facilitator praising the parties' efforts.

CHECK IN

Finally, set a future time — a week, a month, or a few months away — when you will check in with the parties about how their agreement is holding up. Sometimes parties make this part of their agreement, but even if they don't, it is wise to check in. You are most likely to find everyone viewing the conflict as ancient history, and your query will be dismissed with a quick response of "just fine." It may happen, however, that some aspect of an agreement is not working. This gives you and the parties an opportunity to fine-tune the agreement to stave off future problems.

How to Find Help

The conflict resolution method presented here focuses on collaborative conflict resolution techniques. It is often wise to empower people to work through conflicts either with help from a skilled facilitator or on their own before relying upon command processes. Although the collaborative approach is usually far more effective, there are times when in a nonprofit organization, an authoritative person must shoulder the decision. The chief executive and the board chair are the nonprofit leaders vested with this ultimate responsibility and authority. Authoritative decisions are in order in times of emergency, when tough negative decisions have to be made (like layoffs, discharges, and large budget cuts) or when circumstances like harassment or abuse are encountered.

With the authoritative method of decision making (or conflict resolution) comes a price. This form of conflict resolution can deal with substantive issues but cannot handle the relationship conflicts that often accompany them. Organizations are only as effective as the good working relationships of their members. When relationship conflicts remain, further conflict will develop.

Additionally, staff or board members will often be relieved when someone other than they themselves make tough decisions. Yet they often simultaneously harbor negative feelings toward that person, particularly if the resolution does not satisfy their key interests. This can result in eroded interpersonal relationships and less confidence in the leader's judgment. Leaders must at times pay that price, but only after assessing all the options for conflict resolution and consciously choosing the most appropriate method for the situation.

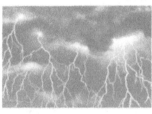

Finding External Help with Conflict Resolution

Conflicts are so common that it is not feasible to get external help each time one occurs. However, you should get external help for complex conflicts or those that no one associated with your organization can facilitate impartially.

A wide range of dispute resolution resources are available. They vary significantly in the types of issues they handle, the time and costs involved, and the amount of control the people in conflict have over the resolution. Following is an overview of litigation, arbitration, mediation, and mediation-arbitration, as well as questions to help you choose a mediator.

LITIGATION

The court system is almost always available as a last resort for settling a conflict, but it is costly and time-consuming. Courts deal most effectively with substantive disputes. At times they take on process conflicts, but never relationship issues. Of the external forms of conflict resolution, litigation gives the people in conflict the least control over the outcome. Attorneys speak for the parties, legal precedents and procedures shape the solutions, and judges or juries make the ultimate decisions. Litigation is usually adversarial, and it tends to escalate already strained relationships — often to irreconcilable levels. The system works particularly well when the issues are substantive, stakes are high, and parties to the dispute will have no future relationship.

Litigated disputes are heard in either criminal or civil courts. Criminal courts handle situations in which people have broken federal or state laws or city ordinances. Civil courts deal with issues of contracts and torts (personal injury claims).

Either court is accessible to nonprofits. However, court dockets are so full that judges are disinclined to deal with matters that can be handled in other venues. Frequently, the process of setting a court date drives an agreement between parties. Attorneys settle many cases through negotiations just before the case comes before the court.

ARBITRATION

In arbitration, individuals in conflict (or their attorneys) make their best case to an arbitrator who weighs the information and determines the resolution. Arbitration can be *binding*, which means there is no recourse to the court system after a decision is made, or *nonbinding*, meaning that the parties may bring their cases to the courts if they are unhappy with the arbitrator's decision.

Arbitration is generally less expensive and time-consuming than litigation. Parties have more control, particularly if they represent themselves. The arbitration system is somewhat less formal and procedurally driven than litigation. However, many arbitrators are attorneys or retired judges, so they often bring much of the litigious context and mind-set to arbitration. Information about arbitration services can be found in the telephone directory and through professional organizations of arbitrators.

MEDIATION

Mediation is the least formal and generally the least expensive external conflict resolution venue. In mediation, parties usually meet face-to-face to discuss and resolve their dispute with the help of a facilitator, called a mediator. (Sometimes two mediators may be called for; when mediating large groups, mediators frequently work in pairs.) On occasion, parties may bring attorneys, but usually mediation is conducted without attorneys present. Mediators facilitate the conflict resolution process but have no decision-making authority. Mediation can be effective in substantive, procedural, relationship-based, and identity-based disputes.

Because it is generally the least expensive process and one that deals with relationships in addition to substantive and procedural issues, it is often helpful to start with mediation. Mediators vary in style and quality, so it is worth doing some research before selecting one.

MEDIATION-ARBITRATION

Mediation-arbitration is a newer avenue of dispute resolution. As its name suggests, it is a hybrid of ar-

bitration and mediation. It generally works like mediation, but if parties cannot come to an agreement, the mediator takes on the role of arbitrator and decides how to resolve the conflict. Many organizations that offer mediation or arbitration offer this hybrid as well, as the same professionals perform this service. The role of an executive or board chair can be similar to mediation/arbitration. If people in dispute cannot agree on a solution, then the chief executive or board chair may ultimately make the decision.

Finding and Hiring a Mediator

Mediators can be found through a variety of sources. Most metropolitan telephone books list community, nonprofit, and for-profit mediation organizations. Some are independent professional mediators or law firms; others are branch offices of large mediation organizations. Word of mouth is often a good way to find a mediator with whom you can work.

Besides cost, consider the following questions when you look for a mediator:

EXPERIENCE

- Does the mediator need special expertise or have to be familiar with certain terminology to work effectively with the parties or the type of conflict?
- Has the mediator dealt with similar situations or conflicts? Is this desirable, or would it be better if he or she had no previous involvement with the issues?

NEUTRALITY

- Should the mediator be someone known to the parties and respected as fair and impartial or should he or she be someone neither party knows?
- Should he or she be from within or outside the community?

ROLE

- How does the mediator view his or her role in administering the mediation process — for example, in handling the meeting logistics, making copies of documents, or word processing?
- What does the mediator expect the parties or organization to do in the process?

PROCESS

- What approach does the mediator recommend?
- Does this approach seem appropriate for your organization and the people involved?

TRAINING

- How much training has the mediator had?
- Who trained the mediator?

FEES AND AVAILABILITY

- Is the mediator available during the period needed?
- What does the mediator charge? If there is an hourly rate, what does it cover? What is the cost of time spent at mediation meetings versus preparation time or travel time?
- Can the mediator estimate the amount of time the project will require?
- Can a price ceiling be negotiated?

In some conflicts, choosing the mediator is a source of contention because each party fears that the mediator might be partial. In such cases, the first step in the conflict resolution process is having the parties work together to select a mediator that all view as acceptable and neutral.

How to Create a Climate for Constructive Conflict

So far this booklet has focused on how a nonprofit leader can help others resolve their conflicts. However, helping others develop their *own* conflict resolution skills will save time and energy and let people use their differences in constructive ways — to gain new perspectives and understanding and to increase productivity and creativity. As conflict resolution skills flourish, divisiveness, interpersonal conflict, and hidden agendas diminish. Turf battles and daily tensions subside. Relationships with the community and service recipients deepen and people become more comfortable with conflict and using it constructively. Of course, like any change in an organization's climate, helping people become skilled at constructive conflict resolution takes time and attention. How can a leader go about creating this conflict-friendly environment? Following are nine activities for creating a climate of constructive conflict in an organization:

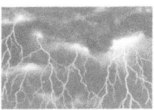

1. Model constructive conflict management practices.

If you have concluded that the conflict resolution methods already discussed are valuable and are committed to "walk the talk," you have already taken the first step to integrating constructive conflict resolution into your organization. Just as your leadership underpins any culture change in your organization, your understanding of conflict and your use of communication and conflict resolution skills are the primary factors in making these a part of your organization's culture. Seeing these methods practiced by the organization's leader is important. Your modeling is essential.

2. Recognize the conflict resolution methods currently in place in your organization and assess their strengths and weaknesses.

Watch carefully and think back to your experiences of conflict within your organization. What are the conflicts about? Do one or two types seem preva-

lent? Who are the parties in conflict? Are the conflicts within the organization or with external constituents? How are the conflicts handled or avoided? Thinking through all of these will give you a picture of the conflict resolution methods currently in use and their relative effectiveness. Note the people whose skills are strong. These are individuals who can take the lead and be models for others in the organization.

3. Enrich other people's understanding of conflict, its challenges, and its benefits.

Bring the idea of creative conflict onto the table. Talk about it. Use this booklet and other resources to help the people in your organization understand its many shapes, the cultural messages around it, people's reactions to it, and the potential it holds for learning and innovation.

4. Help people in the organization gain self-knowledge as a tool for constructive conflict.

There are several instruments that give people insight into their own styles or preferences regarding conflict and communications. These include tools such as the Myers-Briggs Test. Each instrument offers a somewhat different perspective, but all enhance self-knowledge. Use them as part of board orientation and staff development activities; they contribute to people's understanding of themselves and each other.

5. Encourage people in your organization to understand and appreciate differences in their histories, communication styles, decision-making methods, and culture.

Because each person is familiar with only his or her own way of processing information and coming to decisions, it is easy to forget that other people perform these activities differently. It is common for people to view others who have different styles as incompetent, weird, or worse. This misperception is often at the core of workplace conflict. When people with significantly different styles are interdependent, as in the workplace, they can get frustrated or angry that things are not being done in ways that make sense to them. They often begin to psychologically distance themselves from their "different" coworkers.

This is how latent conflict starts. People accentuate their differences, withdraw, and become more judgmental about one another — until some straw breaks the camel's back. The Myers-Briggs Type Inventory (MBTI) is an important and credible tool for understanding one's own perceptions and those of others — and as a result, for preventing the development of these sorts of conflicts.[1]

Information about conflict and conflict resolution skills can become part of your staff and board development activities.

The MBTI, first and foremost, helps people understand their own unique way of processing information and making decisions. It also helps them recognize the different ways in which others do these things. When colleagues understand their own ways of thinking and value other people's ways, some conflicts are eliminated altogether and people are better prepared to use their differences constructively.

The MBTI must be administered by a certified trainer. After the inventory is explained and administered, it is sent to a national center for analysis and then returned to the trainer. He or she will meet once with your organization to administer the inventory and a second time to return the results to participants and explain the results. All individual inventories are confidential and private, so individuals can choose whether to share results. Regardless of whether inventories are shared, participants learn a lot about different ways of thinking.

Besides using the MBTI and related instruments, you can help change the culture of your workplace by helping people recognize the role of family history, ethnic background, and religious heritage in shaping perception.

6. Offer opportunities to learn and use constructive conflict resolution skills.

As you become comfortable and confident as a conflict manager, consider moving your organization to the next stage by empowering others to do the same. Information about conflict and conflict resolution skills can become part of your staff and board development activities. When the people working in your nonprofit have these skills, you will find everyone's time better used. You can actively turn potentially destructive conflict into creative and constructive problem solving.

Communications skills like affirming and restating, mirroring, asking neutral questions, assisting upset people, identifying interests, reframing issues, and limiting, blaming and belittling by using structured statements are helpful to staff at all levels of the organization. Having people practice makes them more likely to use the skills when conflicts arise. These skills can be taught in various ways ranging from formal training sessions to informal discussions at staff or board meetings.

7. Assess organizational systems and practices to understand their contribution to conflict.

Organizational systems can create intentional or inadvertent conflict. Systems of checks and balances that distribute authority and assure quality control can also become arcane and destructive over time. Review systems as your organization grows to ensure the checks and balances do not create conflicts beyond those needed to assure quality.

Areas to review include budgeting and other resource distribution systems (like space and personnel allocations), performance appraisal systems, and program evaluation systems. Personnel policies — especially those regarding hours of arrival and departure, notice of intended absence, and general office decorum — should also be examined. Such rules often remain after the original conditions that triggered their creation have changed.

Most policies and procedures relating to these systems are established to reduce the level of risk to the organization. Therefore, you will need to assess the risk aversion built into these systems and determine how much risk your organization can afford to take. Many conflicts occur when people in gatekeeping roles such as legal, personnel, and finance staff, who frequently need to say no, become enamored of rules and forget to assess the risk of following old rules in a changed environment. Rethinking old policies and procedures needs to be done *with* these staff, but this is no easy task. Gatekeeping is often a form of power, so you need to prepare for potential resistance and power struggles.

8. Encourage and practice supportive communication methods.

The organization's communication style is a key clue to how safe conflict is. This cultural characteristic can range on a continuum from defensive to supportive.

When an organization's chief style of communication is defensive, people anticipate critical responses. In office meetings and conversations, defensive communicators make evaluative and judgmental statements much more often than descriptive statements. They are likely to attribute problems to individuals rather than situations, and to describe problems in terms of the person or group "at fault." In organizations with defensive communication, statements are either ambiguous, leaving loopholes for the intimidated speaker, or else certain and dogmatic, leaving no room for disagreement. Lastly, defensive communication is at work when individuals in groups allude to their status or formal position as justification for a point they are making.

All of these practices make people feel wary as they communicate. The defensive style gives people the clear message that it is unacceptable and unsafe to address conflict directly. As a result conflicts go underground, becoming personal vendettas, hidden agendas, and increasingly fierce turf wars.

In contrast, supportive communication styles tend to be more descriptive than evaluative. Problems are attributed to situations and not to people, statements are clear and leave room for alternatives, and people de-emphasize formal power relationships and communicate with respect and empathy.

Take a fresh look at the types of communication occurring in your organization. You will quickly get a sense of whether your organization's climate is one in which people feel safe to address conflict directly and constructively. While you alone can't change your organization's culture, you can model supportive communications and work to make the organization a safe place for constructive resolution of conflict.

9. Continually work to establish an organizational climate in which change, risk, and conflict are accepted as normal and viewed as stimulants for creativity and learning.

Management gurus preach the benefits of every organization becoming a learning organization, thriving on chaos, managing in white water, and making everyone in the organization entrepreneurs. Of course, these conditions make conflict more likely! Creating an organizational climate in which change, reasonable risk, and conflict are embraced is a wonderful ideal. But doing it takes time, patience, and the willingness to reconsider many traditions. Change is unsettling, and, especially in larger organizations, staff are used to these so-called paradigm shifts blowing in like a nor'easter and blowing out in short order. Don't rush. Slowly and steadily steer your organization toward this ideal culture by making small and easy changes first.

Look long and hard at your organization's *real* incentives and disincentives for bringing conflicts up on the table. What incentives or disincentives are built into your reward and recognition systems, your human resources systems, your performance appraisal systems? Who gets promoted, rewarded, and challenged? How well are your "different" people accepted? Are their ideas really considered? Are people rewarded for taking the risk of addressing conflict, or does the risk simply mean more work for them with no rewards? What happens to risk-takers when they fail? What messages do other members of the organization get about people who are willing to call a conflict a conflict? What messages do people get when they are in conflict? What attitude does the organization have toward outsiders — those people who are either genuinely outside the organization or who are pariahs within the organization?

In addition to considering the formal systems that tell people if conflict, change, and innovation are acceptable, you will want to assess less formal systems. These include how authority is used and the role of friendship and interdependence in your organization.

When people in an organization decide how to address conflict, they combine their understanding of the conflict, their personal ways of dealing with conflict, *and* the unspoken organizational norms and rules about conflict.

Organizations that emphasize formal authority tend to be less hospitable to constructive conflict resolution. When people assess the risk of addressing a conflict, they consider the organization's messages about authority. If these include "don't bother the boss," "make the boss look good at all costs," "do what you're told; don't ask why," or "don't bring bad news — messengers get killed," people will be afraid to point out a conflict, let alone address it. Changing the way authority is viewed and used in an organization is a huge challenge. It often takes a change of leadership to make this happen.

The level of interpersonal friendship and support among people also affects how conflict is handled. In a friendly and psychologically safe environment, people are much more confident that a conflict can be raised and resolved in constructive ways. Though you certainly can't create friendships in the workplace, you can set a tone that supports their development by encouraging informal gatherings and letting employees know that a certain amount of workplace chat is fine. Similarly, you can support interdependence — a sense of group identity in the organization that encourages constructive conflict resolution. When friendship and interdependence thrive, people feel safer about airing conflicts.

· ·

[1] *Some people are wary of the MBTI because it has been misused to pigeonhole people or make excuses for inappropriate or incompetent behavior. However, it can be an excellent tool when administered and analyzed by appropriately trained people. The MBTI has a long history of research and has high credibility as a reliable assessment. In addition, in the past few years the inventory has been further refined, so that its new version, the MBTI Expanded Analysis Report (EAR) gives a deeper look at people's perceiving and decision-making preferences.*

Conclusion

If you were to sit down to write explicit instructions for tying shoelaces, you'd find that careful description would make this simple, automatic task seem more complex than it really is.

In the hope of making the conflict resolution process orderly and explicit, it has been broken down into many discrete steps. However, like tying one's shoe, the action is really quicker, more natural, and far more fluid than the detailed description makes it seem. Conflict resolution applies many management and leadership principles that are already familiar to executives and board chairs. It is a rare individual who rises to these positions without an array of well-developed skills for dealing with people. Like tying one's shoes, most of the conflict resolution process is natural and intuitive. This book is not a rigid, step-by-step recipe for resolving conflict, but rather offers some new understandings and ideas about handling conflict that will augment the wisdom you've earned in a lifetime of dealing with conflict.

Participation and leadership in nonprofit governance is an experience of the democratic process at work. Practicing participative, constructive conflict resolution in nonprofit organizations and

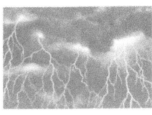

boards can ultimately foster this same practice throughout our society. Nonprofit organizations both mirror and lead our society. On one hand, the factors of change, diversity, limitations, and innovation that challenge nonprofits are reflections of the similar challenges in all parts of our society. On the other hand, nonprofits are the organizations relied upon to take the lead in making societal change, honoring diversity, and developing innovative ways to address weaknesses and limitations in our social systems. As leaders in social change, nonprofit organizations that integrate participative conflict resolution processes into their everyday work life can catalyze their use in the broader community. When people in conflict effectively resolve it, either on their own or with the aid of a facilitator, their experience fosters the confidence to apply these skills and processes in their personal relationships, workplaces, neighborhoods, and communities. Good conflict resolution empowers people, fosters mutual respect and understanding, and enhances creative thinking skills. All of these qualities are essential to keep our democratic institutions — large and small — humane, responsive, and vital.

Suggested Resources

Angelica, Marion Peters. *Resolving Conflict in Nonprofit Organizations: The Leader's Guide to Finding Constructive Solutions.* Saint Paul, MN: Amherst Wilder Foundation, 1999, 192 pages.

This guide's eight-step process helps you identify a conflict, decide whether to intervene, uncover and deal with the true issues, and design and conduct a conflict resolution process. It includes exercises to learn and practice conflict resolution skills, guidance on handling unique conflicts such as harassment and discrimination, and when (and where) to seek outside help with litigation, arbitration, and mediation.

Bailey, Mark. *The Troublesome Board Member.* Washington, DC: National Center for Nonprofit Boards, 1996, 25 pages.

Have you ever been on a board whose progress was continually thwarted by one troublesome member? Have you ever left a meeting frustrated because the efforts to curb this board member's behavior were unsuccessful? Bailey illustrates disruptive board member behavior through case studies and proposes remedies and preventive strategies, as well as tools for the most effective resolution of the problem.

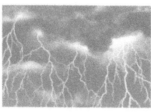

Bilbersten, Bill, and Vijit Ramchandani. *Developing Effective Teams.* Saint Paul, MN: Amherst Wilder Foundation, 1999, 80 pages.

This publication helps you understand, start, and maintain a team. It provides tools and techniques for writing a mission statement, setting team goals, conducting effective team meetings, creating ground rules to manage team dynamics, making decisions in teams, creating team project plans, and developing team spirit. It also shows you how to deal with predictable problems such as conflict, clarifying roles and responsibilities, dealing with performance problems, and communicating between meetings.

Winer, Michael, and Karen Ray. *Collaboration Handbook: Creating, Sustaining, and Enjoying the Journey.* Saint Paul, MN: Amherst Wilder Foundation, 1994, 192 pages.

This handbook shows you how to start a collaboration, set goals, determine everyone's roles, create an action plan, and evaluate the results. It includes a case study of one collaboration from start to finish, helpful tips to avoid pitfalls, and worksheets to keep everyone on track.

About the Author

Marion Peters Angelica is president and founder of Convergences, Inc., a provider of services in conflict resolution and creative problem solving. She is an assistant professor at the Hamline University Graduate School of Nonprofit Management and adjunct professor at St. Mary's College Graduate School of Education, where she teaches conflict resolution and creative thinking.

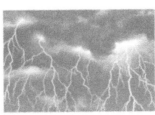

She has more than 20 years' experience with the nonprofit sector as a director, board member, and consultant. She has been a mediator for the Minnesota Department of Human Rights and other organizations, working in the areas of civil rights, juvenile justice, divorce, and community disputes. She holds a Master of Arts from the University of Minnesota, Minneapolis; a Master of Fine Arts from the State University of New York, New Paltz; and is a doctoral student in conflict resolution at the Union Insitute, Cincinnati, Ohio.

Most recently, Marion completed a 14-month tour as a visiting Fulbright scholar in Cyprus, where she worked to strengthen the nongovernmental sector and evaluate the effects of conflict resolution training held there.

Have You Used These NCNB Resources?

Videos

Fearless Fund-Raising: The Video Workshop

Meeting the Challenge: An Orientation to Nonprofit Board Service

Blueprint for Success: A Guide to Strategic Planning for Nonprofit Board Members

Speaking of Money: A Guide to Fund-Raising for Nonprofit Board Members

Building Boards That Work

Books

Measuring Board Effectiveness: A Tool for Strengthening Your Boards

Nonprofit Governance: Steering Your Organization with Authority and Accountability

The Building Board Cycle: Nine Steps to Finding, Recruiting, and Engaging Nonprofit Board Members

The Art of the Story: Case Studies from the Nonprofit Boardroom

The Policy Sampler: A Resource for Nonprofit Boards

Chief Executive Compensation

To Go Forward, Retreat! The Board Retreat Handbook

All Hands On Board: The Board of Directors of an All-Volunteer Organization

Turning Vision Into Reality: What the Founding Board Should Know About Starting a Nonprofit Organization

Nonprofit Board Answer Book

Developing an Ethics Program: A Case Study for Nonprofit Organizations

Leaving Nothing to Chance: Achieving Board Accountability Through Risk Management

Merging Mission and Money: A Board Member's Guide to Social Entrepreneurship

Lobbying, Advocacy, and Nonprofit Boards

A Snapshot of America's Nonprofit Boards: Results of a National Survey

The Board Member's Guide to Fund Raising

The Legal Obligations of Nonprofit Boards

Self-Assessment for Nonprofit Governing Boards

Assessment of the Chief Executive

Developing the Nonprofit Board

Fearless Fund-Raising

Hiring the Chief Executive: A Practical Guide to the Search and Selection Process

Governing Boards

Six Keys to Recruiting, Orienting, and Involving Nonprofit Board Members

Building Board Diversity

Board Members and Risk: A Primer on Protection from Liability

A Corporate Employee's Guide to Nonprofit Board Service

The Nonprofit Board's Guide to Bylaws

The Troublesome Board Member

Creating and Using Investment Policies

A History of Nonprofit Boards in the United States

Board Passages: Three Stages in a Nonprofit Board's Life Cycle

The Board's Role in Maximizing Volunteer Resources

Board Committees Series

Nonprofit Board Committees

The Audit Committee

The Executive Committee

The Nominating Committee

The Finance Committee

The Planning Committee

The Development Committee

The Advisory Committee

Strategic Issues Series

Marketing for Mission

Beyond Strategic Planning

Nonprofit Mergers

Seven Steps to a Successful Nonprofit Merger

How to Manage Conflicts of Interest

Governance Series

1. *Ten Basic Responsibilities of Nonprofit Boards* (available on audiotape and in Spanish and Portuguese booklets)

2. *The Chief Executive's Role in Developing the Nonprofit Board*

3. *Creating Strong Board-Staff Partnerships*

4. *The Chair's Role in Leading the Nonprofit Board*

5. *How to Help Your Board Govern More and Manage Less*

6. *The Board's Role in Strategic Planning* (available on audiotape)

7. *Financial Responsibilities of the Nonprofit Board*

8. *Understanding Nonprofit Financial Statements*

9. *Fund-Raising and the Nonprofit Board Member* (available on audiotape)

10. *Evaluation and the Nonprofit Board*

NATIONAL CENTER FOR NONPROFIT BOARDS

For an up-to-date list of publications and information about current prices, membership, and other services, please call NCNB at 800-883-6262.